Learn French Beading

- Beginner Course -
Technique Reference & Practice Flower Patterns

Bead & Blossom
by Lauren Harpster

© 2020 Lauren Harpster. All rights reserved. No portion of this book may be reproduced or transmitted in any form without permission from the author.

Published in the United States by Bead & Blossom.
BeadandBlossom.com

First Edition, Feb 2020.

Editor: Suzanne Steffenson

All photos in this publication are by Lauren Harpster, except where otherwise noted.

ISBN-13: 978-1-7347209-0-7

Table of Contents

INTRODUCTION
- What are French Beaded Flowers?...... 1
- A Brief History 1
- Using this Course Guide 2
- Accessing the Videos 3

PART 1: GETTING STARTED
- Beads 5
- Wire 8
- Tools 11
- Other Supplies 13
- Stringing Beads onto Wire 13
- Materials for Parts 2 & 3 15

PART 2: TECHNIQUE GUIDE
Lesson 1: Continuous Loops 17
- Centering the Stem Wires 19
- Spacer Beads 20
- Reinforcing Continuous Units 20
- Combining Continuous Units 21

Lesson 2: Continuous Crossover Loops 22

Lesson 3: Continuous Wraparound Loops ... 24
- Round Bottom 25

Lesson 4: Fringe 26
- Twisted Fringe 26
- Wire-Back Fringe 28
- Working with Long Wire-Back Fringes . 29
- Loop Fringes 30
- Fringe Loops 30
- Branching Fringe 31

Lesson 5: Basic Frame 32
- Reverse Wrap 35

Lesson 6: Lacing 36
- Lace-as-you-go 38

PART 3: PRACTICE FLOWER PATTERNS
Lavender 41
  Techniques Used: *Continuous Loops*

Dame's Rocket 49
  Techniques Used: *Continuous Wraparound Loops, Twisted Fringe, Basic Frame, Lacing*

Wild Clematis 57
  Techniques Used: *Continuous Loops, Basic Frame, Lacing*

Black-Eyed Susan 66
  Techniques Used: *Continuous Loops, Continuous Crossover Loops, Basic Frame, Lacing*

PART 4: ARRANGING BEADED FLOWERS 76
- Selecting Flowers 77
- Selecting Beads 77
- Selecting a Vase 78
- Arranging the Bouquet 78
- Alternate Method for Making Bouquets .. 80
- More Sample Arrangements 81

Resources 82

Glossary 83
- Technique Abbreviation List 85

About the Designer 86

Lauren Harpster

Introduction

WHAT ARE FRENCH BEADED FLOWERS?

The term *French Beading* refers to a specific set of techniques used primarily to make flowers. Essentially, French Beading combines beading, wire wrapping, and sculpture into one sparkly package. But not all bead-and-wire flowers are considered "French" beaded. The Victorian Method (also called Continental Method) is often confused with French Beading. How do you tell them apart? The Victorian technique is worked by crossing two wires through a single row of beads and creates parallel rows stacked top to bottom—just like ladder stitch in bead weaving. In French Beading the wire will *usually* pass through beads just once. Rows are worked from the center outward around a central row or loop.

A BRIEF HISTORY

Antique French beaded immortelle restored and photographed by Cynthia Peterson.

When you take up French Beading, you are partaking in an art that is many centuries old. There aren't many historical accounts about it, so very little is known for certain. The best history I've read on the subject, is found in the book "Forever Flower" authored by Swedish beaded flower collector Georg Ragnar Levi. The art probably began during the Renaissance in the 1500's in Italy or France, who were the biggest bead producers at the time. One popular origin story says that peasants gathered beads leftover from embellishing gowns and strung them onto wire, then wrapped to form flowers and leaves. However, it is believed to be more likely that the first beaded flowers were associated with the church and worship. Nuns made and used beaded flowers to make reliquaries and other religious artifacts. In old English "bede" means "prayer". Bede men and women in almshouses were paid to say prayers, using beads strung on wire like a rosary. After a set of prayers were finished, the associated beads were twisted into loops, resulting in something that looked like flowers.

The art reached it's peek in the late 1800's and early 1900's, when these flowers were used to make lavish funeral wreaths, called *immortelles.* They were produced by workers in workhouses, then purchased from shops to display on loved one's graves. Some of these wreaths—and the flowers used to make them—can still be found in antique markets today. Once the *immortelles* became less popular, so did the art.

In the early to mid 1900's a shop called Bonwit and Teller in New York imported flowers made in Italy and France to sell to American customers. But the art of making flowers didn't become popular in the US until the mid 1900's after a woman named Virginia Nathanson bought one of the arrangements and took it apart to discover how they were made. She then wrote a book teaching others how to make them. Other designers and companies followed suit and more books were published. During this time period, beaded flowers were mostly used for home decorations - like arrangements, lampshades, and other ornaments.

We are currently experiencing another upward trend in the popularity of the art. The new era began in the late 1990's and early 2000's. This resurgence began as a new crop of designers—Donna Dickt, Zoe L. Schneider, Dalene Kelly, Carol Benner, among others —published more books that brought the art to another generation.

In short, French Beading has gone through many revivals, with each new generation of artists making exciting breakthroughs that push the art forward! Today there are more artists than ever before developing new techniques and finding creative ways to use old techniques! It's going to be exciting to see how much farther this art form will develop and spread with the advances in technology that makes learning resources easier to produce and distribute than it was for previous generations.

USING THIS COURSE GUIDE

Through my years designing French Beaded Flowers and helping others learn how to make them, I've developed a way of looking at techniques that's a little bit different than other designers and teachers. I've divided the techniques into two categories: *base* and *add-on*. Base techniques can be used alone, or altered by building on top of them with add-on techniques. In contrast, add-on techniques cannot be used alone, but must be used in conjunction with any base. It is my hope that this mix-and-match approach will allow for a greater understanding of French Beading methods and inspire more creative technique combinations. I've divided the techniques into courses based on the skill level and knowledge required to use and understand them.

My *Beginner Course* is all about building the first foundations in the art of French Beading as you will be learning the beginner level base techniques. It is very important to gain a clear understanding of these techniques early on as they are literal foundation blocks. In later courses we will learn more advanced versions of these techniques and the add-on techniques that build on top of them.

- **Part 1** is the "Getting Started" guide. Before making French Beaded Flowers it is very important to understand the materials needed to make them. This section explores tools, beads, wire, and other supplies in great detail, though not all of them will be necessary for this course.

- **Part 2** is the "Technique Guide", which contains six lessons that teach the techniques included in this course. These lessons are important for learning French Beading terms and abbreviations, and how to read French Beading patterns. I like to teach techniques separately from flower patterns because there is so much more I can teach you about an individual technique than what I can cover in a single flower pattern. There are also some variations of the techniques that are not used in the practice patterns, but are included for education and reference. This section is also intended to be a one-stop technique reference so you can quickly look up specific techniques while working with other flower patterns. Each lesson has a video demonstration so you can see the techniques in action, but they also contain picture and written instructions for the techniques.

- **Part 3** contains four wildflower patterns that I've developed specifically for helping you practice the skills you learned in Part 2. The patterns have been written with beginners in mind and contain a high level of detail, so they're a great way to dip your toes into the art. This section is important for seeing practical application of the techniques, reinforcing the ability to read patterns, and learning how to assemble and shape a variety of flowers. I have also made video demonstrations of each of the flowers. While I demonstrate flower parts fully in the videos, I only show techniques as they are used in that particular flower. So you can start with Part 3 if you use the videos, but I do recommend that you go back through the lessons in Part 2.

- **Part 4** will demonstrate how to arrange the flowers from Part 3 to make a wildflower arrangement. I am not a professional florist, but I'd like to share what I've learned. This section is included only in the book and pdf versions of the course.

If you complete the full course you will not only have your own French Beaded wildflower bouquet, but you will also be well prepared to work other flower patterns. When you feel comfortable with these techniques, try out some of the techniques taught in the Intermediate and Advanced Courses on my website.

One thing I want for you to understand is that it's normal to struggle at first. It is very rare for anyone to get the techniques correct and looking perfect on the first try. Please keep trying. Over time your hands will develop a familiarity with the techniques and with wire, and your skills will improve.

- Happy Beading!

Lauren Harpster

Accessing the Videos

This title was made as a reference book that goes along with my Learn French Beading: Beginner Course video series on my YouTube channel. For easy navigation I've created an index page on my website with direct links to all the videos here: beadandblossom.com/beginner-course-links.

Videos in this Course

Part 1: Getting Started

- How to string seed beads onto wire

Part 2: Technique Guide

- Lesson One, Part 1: Continuous Loop Technique Guide
- Lesson One, Part 2: Spacer Beads
- Lesson One, Part 3: Reinforcing & Combining Continuous Units

- Lesson Two: Continuous Crossover Loops Technique Guide

- Lesson Three: Continuous Wraparound Loops Technique Guide

- Lesson Four, Part 1: Twisted Fringe Technique Guide
- Lesson Four, Part 2: Wire-Back Fringe Technique Guide

- Lesson Five, Part 1: Basic Frame Technique Guide
- Lesson Five, Part 2: Reverse Wrap

- Lesson Six: Lacing Technique Guide

Part 3: Practice Flower Patterns

- Lavender Part 1: Bud Units, Bloom Units, & Leaves
- Lavender Part 2: Assembly

- Dame's Rocket Part 1: Stamen, Flowers
- Dame's Rocket Part 2: Leaves
- Dame's Rocket Part 3: Assembly

- Wild Clematis Part 1: Stamen & Petals
- Wild Clematis Part 2: Leaves
- Wild Clematis Part 3: Assembly

- Black-Eyed Susan Part 1: Stamen
- Black-Eyed Susan Part 2: Bud & Flower Petals
- Black-Eyed Susan Part 3: Leaves & Sepals
- Black-Eyed Susan Part 4: Assembly

BeadandBlossom.com

Part 1
Getting Started

Beads

Obviously you can't make beaded flowers without beads. Beads come in a vast variety of shapes, sizes, colors and finishes. The type we use for French Beaded Flowers are round seed beads—also called rocailles. Seed beads are made from glass and have numerical sizes - the larger the number the smaller the bead. In French Beading the most commonly used seed bead size is 11/0. However, I occasionally use larger size 8/0 beads as well as smaller 13/0 and 15/0 seed beads.

There are some colors that are best to buy in bulk, if you are able - green, red, and yellow. These are the colors that I go through the most and it may be cheaper in the long run if you buy them in bulk as some online stores have discounts for large quantities.

Seed Bead Brands

In the world of seed beads there are many different manufacturers, and there are pros and cons to each one. Unlike many of the popular bead weaving techniques, in French beading you can mix different brands in a single piece without negative consequences. Every artist has their own preference for which brands they like to use. You do not have to use the fanciest beads to make beautiful flowers, but do choose the best materials that you can afford. If possible, pick beads that are at least somewhat uniform in shape and size as these will yield the best results.

These are some of the more popular brands:

Photo 1 - *Left: leaf made with Miyuki Delicas. Right: a leaf made in 11/0 round seed beads.*

- **Miyuki®** - Miyuki is a Japanese brand known and loved by bead weavers all over the world. They are best known for the Delica seed beads which are cylinder-shaped beads that are almost exactly the same shape and size. While they can certainly be used, these are not the beads that are used for most patterns, so you'll have to design your own or adjust patterns to fit the different bead size. However, Miyuki also makes round seed beads that I use frequently. These don't have the exact uniformity of Delicas, but that's not necessary for French Beading. What I love most about Japanese beads is that they come in more colors and finishes than Czech or Chinese beads.

- **Toho Beads®**- This is another Japanese company that makes high quality seed beads. Their beads are very uniform in shape and size, though not perfect. They are a little less costly than Miyuki rounds, but still one of the more expensive options. They also have more finishes and colors that aren't available in Czech or Chinese beads.

- **Matsuno®** - Matsuno is yet another Japanese seed bead manufacturer. They produce a line of seed beads called "Dyna-Mites™" for the beading supply store Fire Mountain Gems. They are uniform enough for French Beading, and they are wonderful beads to work with. I do find that they are often more square-shaped than other types of seed beads, but not to the point of it being problematic.

Photo 2 - *Matsuno "Dynamites" (top) compared in shape to Czech Preciosa Ornela (bottom).*

- **Preciosa** - These beads are manufactured in the Czech Republic. This company also owns **Jablonex**, so if you purchase a hank with a Jablonex tag, it's the same. The beads are a little less uniform than Japanese brands, but in French Beading that is no problem. While they do have fewer options for colors than Miyuki and Toho, I can find most of what I need. Czech beads are often sold strung on bundles of strings called "hanks". Each hank of 11/0 seed beads will have 12 strands with approximately 20 inches of beads per strand. Because hanks are strung by length, not weight, the number of grams per hank varies from 30-40 grams, depending on what finish you purchase as some finishes add or remove weight from the beads. However each full hank will cover the same surface area because the strung length and number of strands will be the same.

Photo 3 - *a hank of Czech seed beads.*

Photo 4 - *a leaf made with Chinese beads.*

- **Chinese Beads** - These are the cheapest option, but they are cheap for a reason. They tend to be very irregular in size and shape, which can cause problems if you are following patterns with bead counts. Leaves and petals made from the same pattern may not end up the same size. They create a lot of extra surface texture due to the irregular bead shapes. In addition, the finishes aren't the same quality as Czech and Japanese beads—meaning they aren't as stable and may wear off or fade more quickly. Take care when cleaning these beads!

Seed Bead Finishes

Seed beads come with many different types of finishes. Each type of finish creates a different effect on the bead, and in turn can have a great impact on the style and aesthetics of your flower. Using certain finishes can help mimic leaf or petal textures, or help bring attention to a certain part of the design. Here are just a few tips to get you started:

- If you want to recreate the look of a waxy leaf or petal you might try using opal or opaque luster beads.
- Transparent matte and opaque matte beads have a velvety appearance.
- Using an opaque bead for markings on a leaf or petal made with a different bead finish will make the markings pop.
- When you make a flower with multiple layers of petals, or a large arrangement of flowers using one bead color, the beads tend to blend together, making it look like a mass of beads. To help the eyes distinguish between individual petals, try using a different bead finish of the same color, or a lighter or darker shade of the same color for just the outer rows.

Photo 5 - *Some examples of bead finishes. Left to Right: Transparent, Transparent Luster, Transparent Rainbow (AB), Transparent Matte, Opaque, Opaque Luster, Opaque Rainbow (AB)*

Every artist has their own preferences for which bead finishes to use. Everyone observes and recreates details in their own way. Sometimes the color you need for a specific flower is only available in certain finishes. Whatever your preference and circumstance, I recommend playing around with different seed bead finishes, and combinations of finishes, to see what effects you can make. There is no right or wrong here, only personal preference.

Generally, higher quality beads will have nicer and longer lasting finishes, but there are some types that are less stable than others. Some colors can only be applied to glass using dye on the surface of the bead. These dyed beads are prone to fading, either over time or from exposure to sunlight or chemicals. However, most of the brighter purple and pink beads are dyed, so they can be hard to avoid. The silver inside silver-lined beads will tarnish over time and turn black. How long that takes will depend on your environment and how you store them. To keep them bright longer, keep them sealed in a dry, air-tight container. The metallic finish on galvanized beads is also prone to rubbing off and fading, though some brands have produced a more durable galvanized finish that lasts longer. All these finishes also have issues with skin contact causing them to rub off or fade. Since most French Beaded Flowers aren't worn, this is only a problem while making them, or if you use your flowers to make jewelry. However, just because the finishes are unstable doesn't mean you should never use them. Just treat them kindly, and do whatever you can to prolong their life. Keep them out of the sunlight and moist environments. Consider displaying them in glass domes, and only clean them with a damp cloth.

About Bead Counts

One thing that sets French Beading apart from other types of beading is that we don't count beads per row most of the time. This is because French Beading patterns are made to work with a variety of seed bead brands. However, beads made by different manufacturers may not all be the same size. Even if they are all an 11/0, they may not be the same stringing length. Czech and Japanese beads, which are the most popular type of seed beads used in French Beading, are not always the same stringing length from one bead lot to the next. So if you are using a different brand of beads than the designer you may use more or less beads. There is also going to be some variation based on the technique of the individual artist.

Some patterns may use bead counts for the first row or loop, while others use a measurement. Measurements are usually more accurate when switching from one brand to another, but it's not always possible to design with nice, even measurements. Some techniques just work best when you have either an odd or even number for the starting rows, so you will see bead counts from time to time. In my patterns, I only use counts if the number is less than 20. After that length, a bead or two added to the starting rows won't make a great deal of difference, so you can round up to the nearest "clean" measurement.

Getting Started

Patterns will give you an approximate amount of beads needed to complete the project. Always purchase more!

Some patterns will give the amount of beads as a number of hanks while others will tell you an amount in grams. The amount of beads per gram or per hank will vary depending on the cut and finish. Sometimes a pattern will give the amount in hanks while you are purchasing in grams, or vise versa, so you will need to convert. The conversions below are for size 11/0 round seed beads.

- *Hanks to Grams - calculate the grams needed by assuming a hank has 40 grams of beads. So 2 hanks = 80 grams.*
- *Grams to Hanks - calculate the number of hanks needed as though a hank has 30 grams of beads. In this case, 80 grams = 2.7 hanks.*

This will help cover all bases to ensure you have enough beads to complete the project. You might end up with extra beads, but that's better than not having enough!

Working With Multiple Bead Colors

With most techniques, if you are only working with one color of beads you can pre-string all of the beads onto the wire and work from the spool without having to cut any wire. This helps reduce wire waste and prevents any accidental wire shortages.

Some flower patterns will require you to work with multiple colors of beads on one leaf or petal. Because the number of beads per row varies from one person to the next, the exact bead counts for each color will also vary. Generally, it is not wise to pre-string beads when working with multiple colors unless you want them to fall randomly within the petal. Instead, once you reach the point where you switch colors, you will cut enough bare working wire to finish the piece and add colors to the wire as needed. Because of the fluctuation in bead counts by bead brand and individual beaders, it is difficult to write patterns with complex shading designs. If you are working with a pattern that uses bead counts you may need to adjust them a little. That said, some easy shading patterns may work with bead counts, especially if the markings are at the beginning or end of a row.

······ WIRE ······

Wire makes up the skeletal support system for French Beaded Flowers. There are two basic types of wire that we use to make flowers: the actual leaf and petal component wires, and the stem wires on which the flowers are mounted.

Component Wires

The type of wire we use to make flower parts is called copper-core wire. As the name suggests, this wire has a core made of copper that is either coated with a coloring, or plated with another metal. This type of wire can withstand a lot of bending, can be easily molded into shape, holds shape well, and is still strong enough to support flower pieces.

In some countries you can find copper core wire that has colored enamel coatings. If you can find it in colors, and can afford purchasing many colors, I do recommend using it. Using matching colored wire not only enhances the color of the beads (if using transparent or semi-transparent beads), but it also helps conceal any exposed wires. However, if you can't find wires with colored coatings, don't worry too much. Many artists use only silver colored wire.

Photo 6 - *spools of copper wire*

Stem Wires

For the flower stems and leaf branches you will primarily be using florist stem wires, which are made from steel. These types of wire can be found easily in the floral department of just about any craft store. But they are usually limited to 18 inches long, and the sizes only go up to 16 gauge. The most common gauge you will use for flower stems is 16 gauge. If you need a thicker wire for a heavier flower, you can bundle multiple of these stem wires together.

You can also purchase coils of galvanized steel wire from the hardware store. Not only is this wire perfect for heavier flowers since it comes in thicker gauges, it is especially helpful for very tall flowers since it comes in one long length that you can cut to size.

Photo 8 - *coil of galvanized steel wire*

Photo 7 - *Florist stem wire*

About Wire Gauges

In the US (and a few other countries) we use gauges to describe wire sizes. The larger the number, the thinner the wire. The gauges I use the most are 24 and 30. A small spool of 30 gauge wire will go far, but I buy many of colors of 24 gauge in bulk - green, red, gold, and white. The other sizes and colors I buy as needed for specific projects.

Below is a list of the wire gauges you will use in French Beading, the comparable metric sizes, and what they are used for. Some companies round the metric numbers a little differently, but they should be similar to these measurements.

Gauge	Metric	Used for
30-32 gauge copper core	0.25 - 0.2 mm	lacing flower pieces, flower assembly, tiny flower parts
28 gauge copper core	0.32 mm	flower assembly, small flower parts (like stamen)
26 gauge copper core	0.4 mm	very small flower petals, leaves, and stamen. Assembling heavy flowers, trees, or wreaths.
24 gauge copper core	0.5 mm	most petals and leaves, extra unit support wires
22 gauge copper core	0.64 mm	extra large flower petals and leaves, extra support wires
20 gauge florist stem wire	0.8 mm	Unit support wires
18 gauge florist stem wire	1.02 mm	Unit support wires, stems for very small flowers and leaves
16 gauge florist stem wire/ galvanized steel	1.3 mm	Unit support wires, stem wires for standard sized flowers and leaves.
14 gauge galvanized steel	1.6 mm	Stem wire for heavy flowers, wreath frames, armatures
12 gauge galvanized steel	2.06 mm	Stem wire for extra heavy flowers, wreath frames, armatures

Getting Started

NOTE: *The "Unit Support Wires" that are mentioned in the chart on the previous page are extra wires added in to a petal or leaf to add extra support. This is not taught in this course, since they are used mostly for very large or heavy components, which we aren't doing in the Beginner Course. However, if you'd like to learn about them, you can find a tutorial on my website.*

About Wire Measurements

You will sometimes work with a pattern that tells you to measure and cut a specific amount of wire. Cut more wire! The exact amount used will vary from one artist to the next, so cut a little extra at least the first few times you make a component.

Some patterns will tell you how much wire you need to purchase, but not all do. If there is an amount listed, always buy more.

Wire Brands

Just like beads, choosing which wire brand to use is a personal decision, but I'd like to at least share my experiences and preferences to help guide you in picking which ones you would like to work with. Whatever type you choose, I highly recommend to buy the best wire that you can afford. The quality of the wire you use will determine how long and how well the flowers will hold up to time and being handled.

• Paddle Wire

Paddle wire, or florist wire, is the cheapest type of wire on the market that can be used in French Beaded Flowers. It only comes in four colors - green, silver, white, and sometimes black - so your options are limited. You can find this in the floral department of your local craft or hobby store.

This is not my favorite wire to work with. I have broken it almost every time I've tried it, and the color coating often flakes or peels off. It is not copper wire, but actually made of steel, which becomes brittle more readily than copper when it's bent and wrapped. It is also a little stiffer than other types of wire in the same sizes. However, this is just my experience with the wire. There are artists who use it exclusively, and it won't cost much to give it a try.

Photo 9 - *Paddle wire*

• Zebra Wire™

Zebra wire is fairly inexpensive and decent quality. If you have a tight budget, this wire may be a good option for you. They have a small variety of colors and gauges.

I used this wire a lot in the past, and I was happy with it. I've never had their 24 gauge break on me and the color coating holds up well to wrapping, bending, and coiling, though it can rub off on your fingers a little. However, I don't recommend the silver colored wire. Everything I've ever made with it has tarnished after just a couple years. Their "Gold" is actually made from brass, not copper, and is not suitable for French Beading.

The 24 gauge wire in this brand is a little stiffer than other brands' 24 gauge wire. But their 26, 28, and 30 gauge wires are softer and more prone to breaking than the higher end brands.

Photo 10 - *Zebra wire*

- **Parawire™**

    Parawire's round copper core craft wire is a much loved favorite among French Beaders, myself included. It is a little more expensive than the previous options, but this is excellent wire, and well worth the cost. They have a large variety of colors to choose from. They even have pure white, though it is softer than other colors of 24 gauge wire. Their wire is tarnish and chip resistant. It is one of my favorites and I use it almost exclusively. You can email Parawire to order bulk spools of wire. I do this especially for colors that I go through quickly, like gold, red, green, and white.

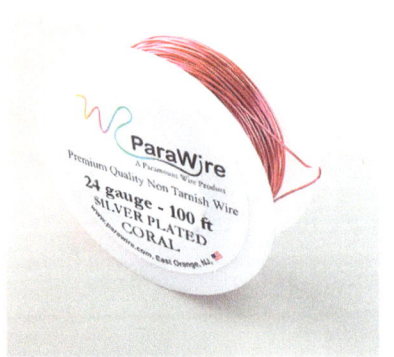

Photo 11 - *Parawire*

- **Artistic Wire®**

    Artistic Wire is another high quality wire option for copper-core wire, and another favorite for French Beaders. It is the most expensive option, but you get what you pay for. It is tarnish and chip resistant, and their finishes hold up very well. While I don't believe it's "better" than Parawire, they do have colors that Parawire does not currently offer. They even have a "Pearl Silver" and "White", which are both actually off-white, creamy colors, though they still work well with white beads. The only downside to Artistic Wire is the cost. We French Beaders go through a lot of wire, so it can add up very quickly.

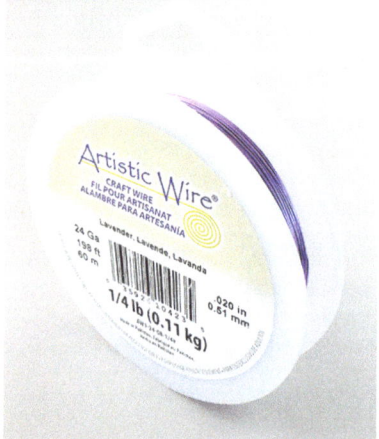

Photo 12 - *Artistic Wire*

- **Scientific Wire**

    Scientific Wire is a company in the UK that produces colored copper wires. I imported some into the USA just so I could test it. The wire itself is comparable to Parawire in quality and feel, however, the clear coating over the colors peeled off while I was twisting and wrapping, so I can't rate it quite as high. The prices are very reasonable and they do have lots of colors to choose from. From my experience and the experiences of others, I consider this to be a great source of wire for those in or around the UK.

Photo 13 - *Scientific Wire*

・・・・・・ TOOLS ・・・・・・

Wire Cutters

You will want some regular side-cutting or flush wire cutters. These can be found at just about any jewelry supply store. Finger nail clippers work well for cutting the copper wires used for making petals, and they are cheap to replace.

You will also want heavier duty cutters for cutting the steel florist stem wires. There are usually stem wire cutters in the floral department of your local craft store, near the packages of stem wires. Using regular wire cutters on the thicker steel stem wires will make them wear out more quickly, or break altogether. They will all wear out over time, but nicer more expensive ones will last longer, especially if you take good care of them.

As you dive deeper into French Beading and start making heavier flowers, you will want some extra heavy duty wire cutters that can cut at up to 12 gauge steel for cutting the thicker galvanized steel wire that comes in coils. These cutters can be found at a hardware store.

Pliers

Flat nosed pliers are nice to have to help bend wires or grab them to pull through, though you will usually do the wrapping with just your fingers. Flat nylon jaw pliers will help smooth out your wires if you get any kinks. If you are using your flowers to make jewelry, some needle nosed or round nosed pliers will come in handy.

Photo 14 - *Wire cutters (top left), stem cutters (middle left), pliers (bottom left), extra heavy duty galvanized steel cutters (right).*

Photo 15 - *Small and large bead spinners*

Bead Spinners

If you plan to make French Beading one of your long-time hobbies, you might want to invest in a bead spinner to help load beads onto the wire. I prefer the wooden hand spun ones over the electric ones as you can control the speed, they aren't noisy, and you won't have to keep buying batteries. However, the electric type are very helpful for beaders with arthritis or other conditions that affect the hands. Bead spinners work best when they are half-way to two-thirds full, so I recommend starting with a smaller sized bead spinner. You can always add more beads to it when the bowl gets low.

Other Tools

- Scissors
- A measuring tape or ruler
- Some plastic bags to store and organize your wire spools, beads, or works in progress
- A small funnel to help you move beads from the spinner back into their containers
- A carrying case (optional - if you plan on taking your supplies anywhere)
- A beading mat or tray to put under the bead spinner or work area - this helps catch any beads that fly out and makes clean up for accidental spills much easier.

Learn French Beading: Beginner Course

•••••• OTHER SUPPLIES ••••••

Along with beads, wire, and tools, there are also a variety of other supplies that will be used frequently in French Beading.

Stem Finishing Supplies

- **Floral Tape** - normally comes in green, white, and brown in your local craft store's floral department, but can be found in many other colors online.
- **Embroidery floss** - Traditionally, French beaded flower stems are wrapped in floss, though it is not a requirement. You can use just about any type of embroidery floss that you like, but the most commonly used types are the regular cotton/poly floss you find at craft stores, and *untwisted flat* silk floss. Experiment with different types to see what you prefer.
- **Glue** - If you plan on using embroidery floss to wrap your stems you may sometimes need some glue to secure the ends of the floss. I like Fabri-Tac™, though I'm sure there are many glues that would work well for this application. *But the only time I use any type of glue to actually assemble flowers is for accessories!* For accessories that require gluing, I use E6000® or a jewelry-grade epoxy. Super glues may react negatively with some bead finishes, so it's best to steer clear.

Photo 16 - *Embroidery floss and floral tape*

Planting and Arranging Supplies

- Floral Clay, or *non-hardening* modeling clay
- Floral Foam
- Plaster, synthetic water, or resin (for potting)
- Decorative moss, grass, pebbles, and other types of camouflage to cover the clay/plaster/foam
- Marbles or pebbles to weigh down the bottom of a vase or conceal clay/plaster/foam
- Pots and vases (Check your local thrift store! I find some interesting and inexpensive vessels there.)

Photo 17 - *Non-hardening clay, plaster, vase filler marbles, floral foam*

•••••• STRINGING SEED BEADS ONTO WIRE ••••••

Stringing beads onto wire is something you'll be doing a lot of with French Beading, and I promise you don't want to do it one-by-one if you can avoid it. There are two basic methods for transferring them to wire: directly from the hank, or with a bead spinner.

Getting Started

From the Hank

If you purchase beads that come strung on hanks, there's a very simple and easy way to string beads. This method doesn't require any special tools, so it's a great option for those just starting out who don't want to invest a lot in tools and supplies just yet. To string, remove one of the threads from the top knot, insert the end of your wire into the beads and remove them from the thread while sliding them onto the wire (**Photo 18**). This works best when you keep the thread and line of beads as straight as possible so you can pass through more beads at once. You can, alternatively, remove both ends of one strand from the top knot, and tie a knot around the last bead at one end so it can act as a stopper bead. Then insert the wire into the beads on the other end of the thread and slide it through. This is especially helpful since hanks tend to start falling apart as you remove more threads.

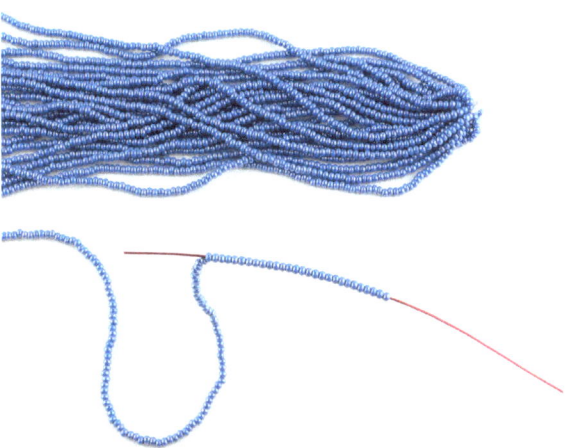

Photo 18 - *stringing beads from a hank*

There are a few downsides to this method. Sometimes Czech beads have smaller holes or are strung on thicker threads, so the standard 24 gauge (.5 mm) wire doesn't always fit through while they're still on the thread. Also, when working with multiple colors of beads or with certain techniques, you sometimes have to string beads and then remove beads as needed to fit. You can't put the beads back on the threads easily, so when it comes time to add more of that color to the wire, you'll have to re-string the loose beads by hand. Finally, some beads just don't come on hanks, and hanks aren't sold in every country, so it's not always an option.

Using a Bead Spinner

This method will require a little bit of practice, but once you get it, it's a fast way to string beads that come loose or when stringing from the hank doesn't work. This is my preferred method to string beads, and I usually do cut hanks apart and put the beads in a spinner.

First, fill the bowl of the bead spinner so it is ½ to ⅔ full. if the bowl is more than ⅔ full, you will get more beads flying out of the bowl and into the void. Make sure you have a nice flush cut on the end of the wire, then bend it into a hook shape. Insert the wire so it's at a slight angle from the beads, but with no wire touching any part of the bowl. The tip of the wire should be pointing toward the outer edge of the bowl (**Photo 19**). Hold the wire with one hand so the tip is just skimming the surface of the beads, then with your other hand, use the spindle in the center to spin the bowl (**Photo 20**). If you are right-handed, it's easiest to have the wire in the right side of the bowl, and spin the bowl counter-clockwise.

Photo 19 **Photo 20**

Learn French Beading: Beginner Course

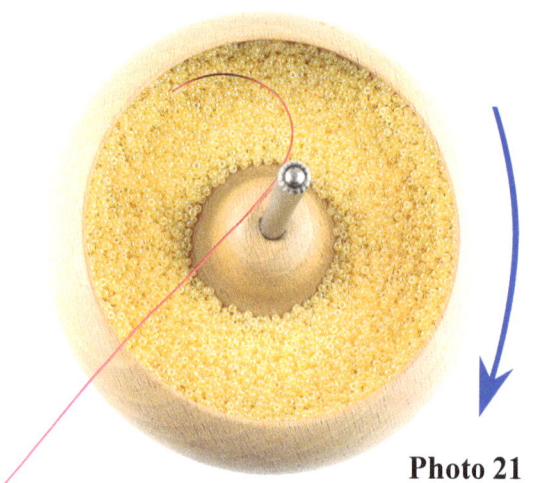

Photo 21

If you are left-handed, try putting the wire in the left side of the bowl, and spinning clockwise (**Photo 21**).

If you're having trouble getting beads onto the wire, play around with the angle and position of the wire and shape of the hook until beads fly on easily.

There is a downside to this method other than requiring a little bit of practice to learn. As the fill line gets lower, the beads will string more slowly, so you may need to fill the bowl with *more* beads than required for the pattern if you want to string quickly.

······ MATERIALS FOR PARTS 2 & 3 ······

I do recommend working through the technique lessons in Part 2 to practice the techniques before making flowers that you'll want to keep. Generally, it just doesn't go well or look nice the first few times you try a new technique. To work through the technique lessons instead of just using them for reference, you will need these supplies:

PART 2 WIRE: Get one spool of each size in any color.
- 24 gauge (.5 mm) copper core wire
- 28 gauge (.315 mm) copper core wire
- 30 gauge (.25 mm) copper core wire

PART 2 BEADS:
- 11/0 round seed beads - Get at least a couple hanks (or somewhere around 80 grams) so you'll have plenty to practice with. The color does not matter.

PARTS 2 & 3 TOOLS:
- Wire cutters
- Stem cutters
- ruler/tape measure
- bead spinner (optional)
- Scissors

NOTE: The practice flower patterns in Part 3 have individual lists of beads and wires. However, I wanted to note that you don't have to purchase each of the listed sizes in all the colors listed if you aren't ready to invest that much into French Beading just yet. Instead, you can work all of the patterns in just silver colored copper core wire in the sizes listed. Then you can purchase a spool or two of each size and use the same wires for all the flowers. The patterns use 24 gauge (.5 mm), 26 gauge (.4 mm), 28 gauge (.315 mm), and 30 gauge (.25 mm).

Part 2
Technique Guide

Lesson One: Continuous Loops

Terms to Remember
- Continuous Loops
- CL
- Continuous
- Tail Wire
- Working Wire
- Spacer Beads
- Unit Stem Wire
- Reinforce

Continuous Loops (sometimes abbreviated as **CL**) are the simplest technique used in French Beading. Simply put, they are a series of beaded loops. Whenever you see the word **Continuous** in a technique name, it means that you will be making multiple petals, sepals, leaves, etc. on the same length of wire. There are several continuous techniques that you will learn in this course.

The way patterns are written or formatted may differ from one designer to the next, but they will all have the same bits of information. Every pattern should tell how many units to make, how many loops are in each unit, and how many beads are in each loop. Some patterns may use a measurement rather than a numerical bead count. A pattern using Continuous Loops will look something like this:

Make 1: 5x CL using 1 ¼ inches (3.2 cm) beads each

Translation: make one of these Continuous Loop units for the flower. The unit will have 5 loops, and each loop needs 1 ¼ inches of beads. If the instructions said "Make 2", for example, then you would complete the pattern once and cut that unit from the wire spool, then make a second identical unit on a separate length of wire.

Photo 1

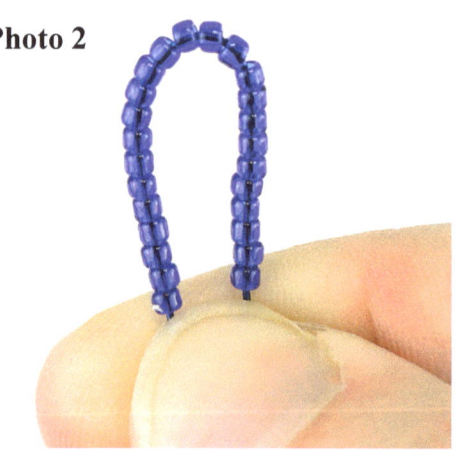

Photo 2

For this exercise, use 26 or 24 gauge wire with approximately 1 gram of size 11/0 seed beads. Follow the sample pattern above.

1. String all the beads onto the wire, leaving the wire attached to the spool.

2. At the beginning of the wire, leave a small section of the wire bare before making any loops - usually 2-3 inches (5 - 7.6 cm) unless the pattern states a specific length. This **tail wire** will become part of the **unit stem wire,** which will be used to attach the loops to the flower's stem wire during assembly. The other end of the wire, which is strung with beads and feeds directly to the spool is referred to as the **working wire**. This is the wire you'll use to make the loops.

3. Measure 1 ¼ inch (3.2 cm) of beads from the spool (**Photo 1**).

4. Fold the beads into a loop, keeping tension on the beads with your thumb and forefinger so gaps don't appear between the beads (**Photo 2**).

5. Keep your fingers in place holding onto both wire ends below the loop of beads. Then twist the loop one to two full rotations (2-4 twists - I usually do 3 twists.) with the other hand to twist the wires together below the loop (**Photo 3**). You should not twist the wires down any further unless specifically instructed to do so in a pattern.

Photo 3

Lesson One: Continuous Loops

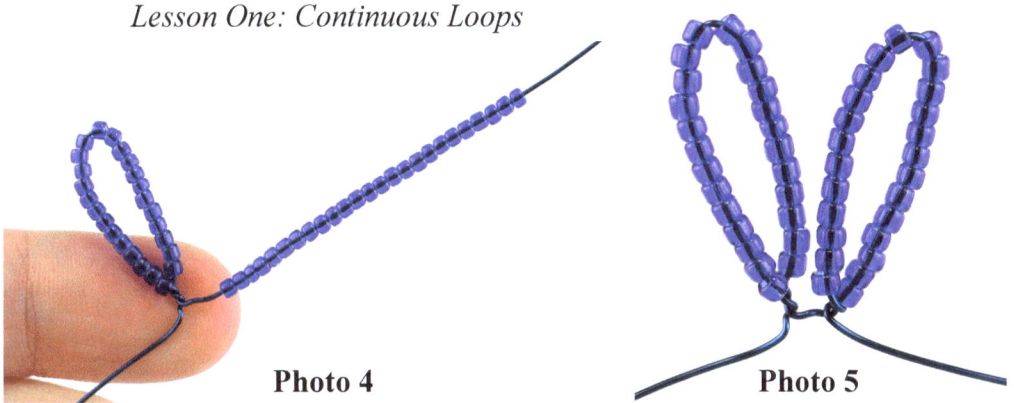

Photo 4   Photo 5

6. Measure out another 1 ¼ inch (3.2 cm) beads on the working wire for the next loop. (**Photo 4**)

7. Leave a small gap in the wire between loops - around ³⁄₁₆ of an inch (4.8 mm). Form the beads into a loop by twisting the wires beneath two full rotations (**Photo 5**).

NOTE: *Making loops too close together makes them bunch up on top of each other (which you usually don't want). In contrast, leaving too much space will make the unit too wide and the petals too far apart. Leaving too much space will make the central hole in the middle of the unit too large for the flower center.*

8. Continue making loops until there are five total (**Photo 6**). The petals should be in a somewhat straight line.

9. Most of the time, you'll close this line of loops into a circle. To close it, cross the working wire over the first loop (**Photo 7**). Wrap around the twisted wires below this loop once, then bring the working wire to the underside of the unit. After closing the unit, measure the working wire to 2 or 3 inches (5 - 7.6 cm) and cut from the spool.

10. Twist the beginning tail wire and working wire together on the underside of the unit (**Photo 8**). You don't need to twist all the way down, just an inch or so (2.5 cm) will do. Try to keep the twists nice and smooth. Any lumps in this wire will show on the flower stem.

The "face" of the finished CL unit is shown in **Photo 9**.

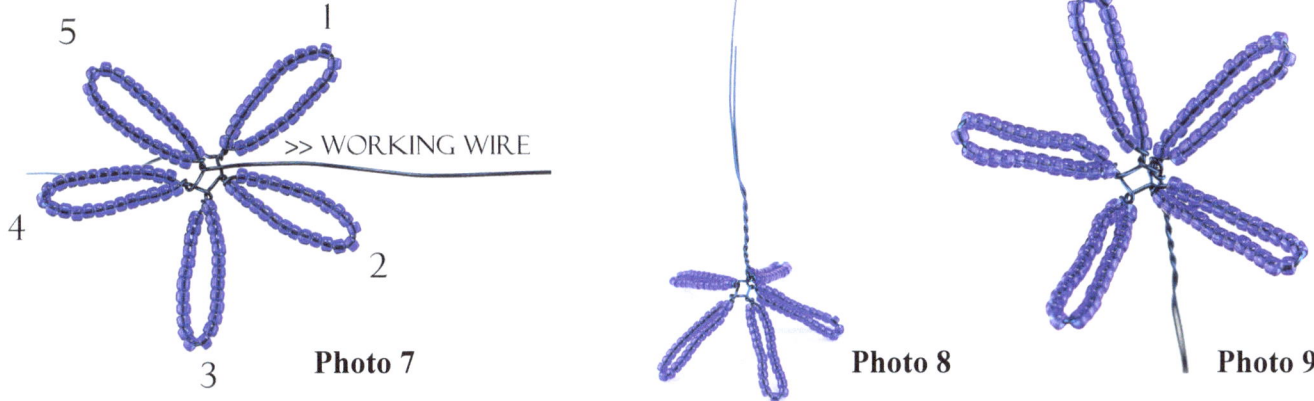

Photo 7   Photo 8   Photo 9

The twisted wire beneath the petal unit is called the **Unit Stem Wire.** *Do not cut it off! You'll need it to attach the petals to the flower stem. But do trim the two wires to different lengths. This will ensure that the wires will end at different points on the flower stem, which helps the stem taper down in width slowly rather than at all once.*

Lauren Harpster

Learn French Beading: Beginner Course

Centering the Stem Wires

You will often be making units with a larger number of loops, which may need to be closed differently. As you can see in **Photo 10**, after wrapping the working wire around the first petal to close the unit it leaves both the tail and working wires off to the side. With fewer petals this isn't a problem since the wires are still near the center of the unit. With a larger number of loops it pulls the stem wires further away from the center, which makes it harder to center the unit on the flower stem. It also means the far side across from the wires doesn't have as much support and may be more inclined to droop. To fix this, we need to re-position the wires so they are closer to the center. You won't *always* need to do this. When in doubt, wait until assembly. Then when it's time to add that unit, test it on the stem to see if the wire position allows for the unit to be centered on the flower stem. If not, remove it and center the wires.

NOTE: *A pattern may or may not tell you to center the unit stem wires as I'm not sure other designer use this concept, so it will largely be up to your own personal judgment.*

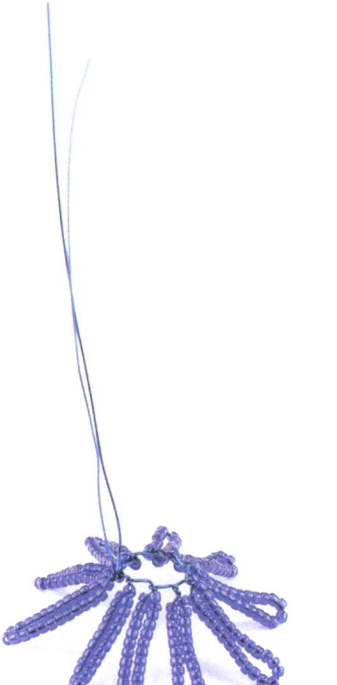

Photo 10

1. Cross the working wire over the first petal and wrap around it once, just like you would with a smaller unit.

2. Then cross the working wire over the bottom (or top, it doesn't matter which) of the unit and wrap it around a petal on the opposite side (**Photo 11**).

3. Bring the working wire back to the underside of the unit and the tail and working wires should be on opposite sides, as shown in **Photo 12**.

4. To finish, bring both wires together in the center and twist them together to make a centered unit stem wire (**Photo 13**).

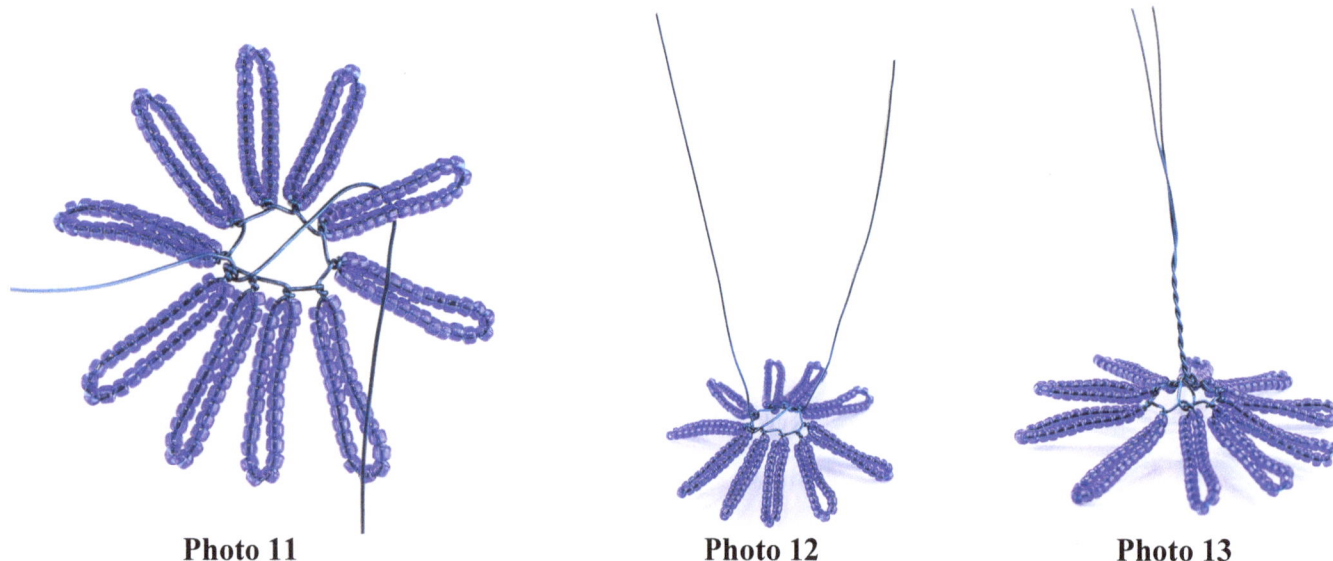

Photo 11   **Photo 12**   **Photo 13**

Lesson One: Continuous Loops

Spacer Beads

You may come across a pattern that calls for the use of **Spacer Beads**. These are beads that are left on the wire between loops. Their primary purpose is to conceal wire that might otherwise be visible on the face of a flower. Spacer beads can be used with any continuous technique.

Simply count out the number of Spacer Beads required onto the working wire and position them directly after the first loop, then measure the beads for the second loop. Because one purpose of a spacer bead is to conceal the wire, leave just enough wire space to make the twists. This way, the next loop will sit directly beside the spacer beads. **Photos 14-16** show a continuous loop unit that uses two Spacer Beads between loops and after the last loop.

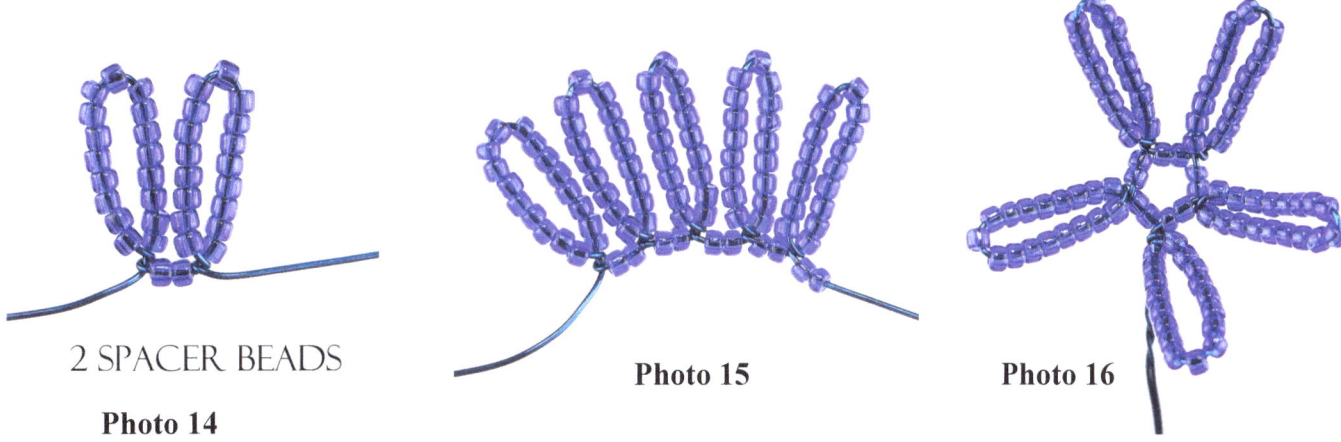

2 SPACER BEADS

Photo 14   **Photo 15**   **Photo 16**

Reinforcing Continuous Units

Sometimes larger continuous units will need extra support so the petals don't become floppy. To reinforce them, close the unit into a circle by wrapping around the first loop. Then continue wrapping or weaving the working wire around the twisted wires below each of the individual petals until you reach the starting point again. This will not only add extra support to individual petals, but also makes the whole unit more sturdy. If necessary, you can weave the wire around again, which will start to form a wire mesh underneath the flower. See **Photos 17 - 20.** You can reinforce any continuous technique.

NOTE: *This is not a technique that I learned from books or other designer's tutorials and I am not sure if anyone else even uses it at all in their patterns. So, just like centering the unit stem wire, it will be up to your own judgment.*

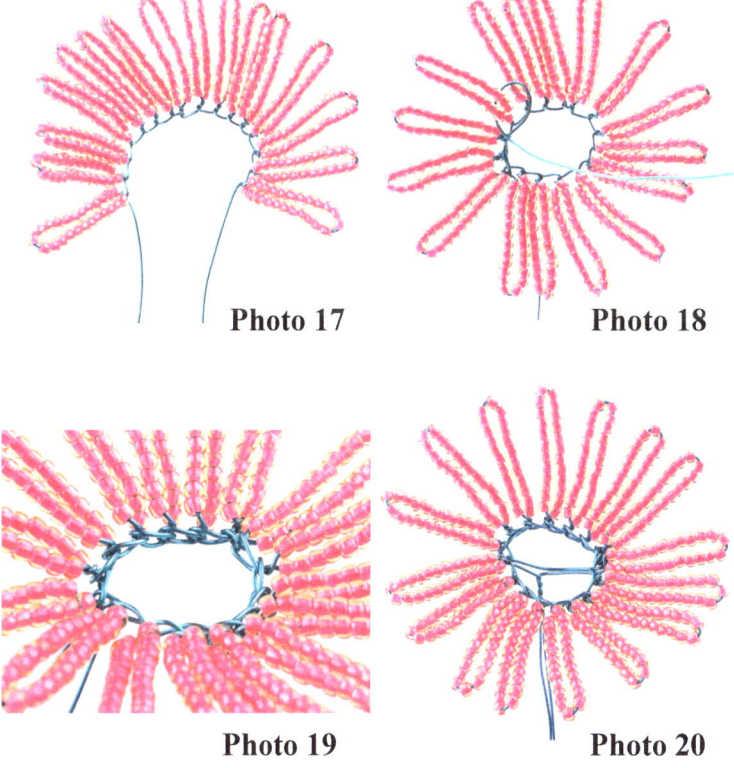

Photo 17   **Photo 18**

Photo 19   **Photo 20**

Lauren Harpster

Combining Continuous Units

Sometimes two unit stem wires aren't enough to support petal units made with continuous techniques. In this case, it's possible to divide the unit into two separate pieces and then weave them together to both reinforce the wires between petals, and add a couple extra stem wires to support the whole unit. This process is very similar to Reinforcing Large Units, and will work with any continuous technique.

1. While making the units, leave the working end of the wires a little longer than normal. The exact length will depend on the size of the unit.
2. Weave the working wire on one unit around each of the petals in the second unit. (**Photo 21**)
3. Weave the working wire on the second unit around the petals in the first unit. (**Photo 22**) *You can weave around again with both wires if necessary.*
4. Twist the working wires of each unit together with it's own starting tail. (**Photo 23**)
5. Twist the four wires together near the center if necessary.

NOTE: *This is another one of those things that patterns may or may not tell you to do. If you ever feel it necessary, do it.*

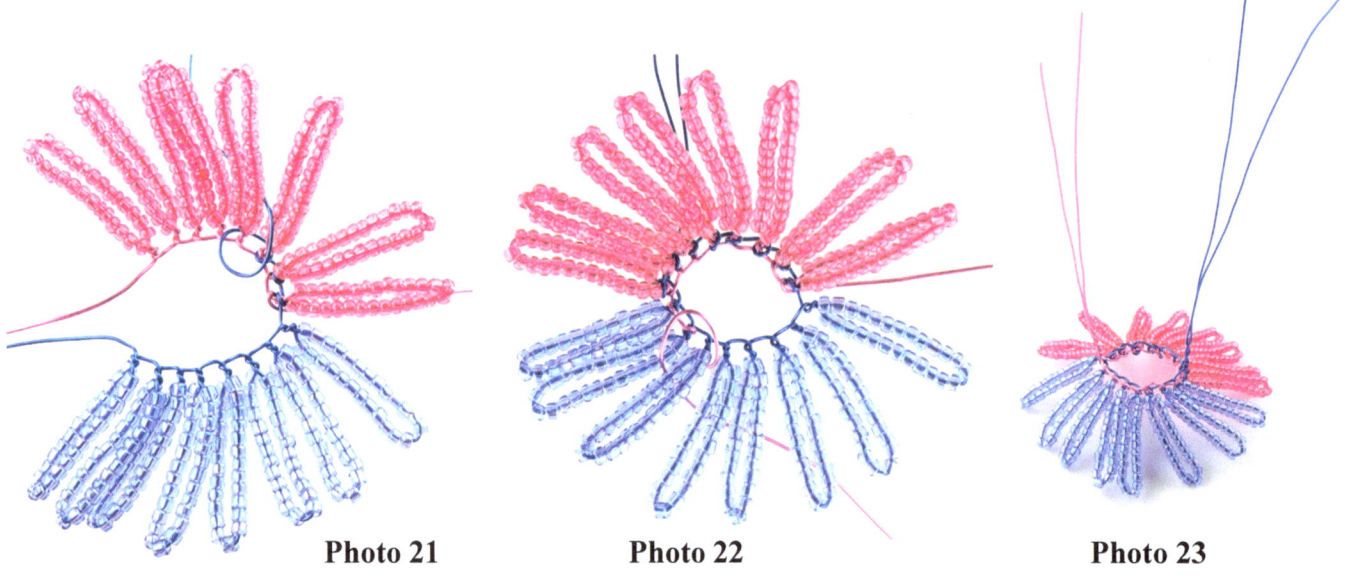

Photo 21   Photo 22   Photo 23

Lesson Two: Continuous Crossover Loops

Terms to Remember
- Crossover Loops
- CCL
- Starting Loop

Continuous Crossover Loops (sometimes abbreviated as **CCL**) is usually continuous, but the loops can be used individually for buds or stamen.

The standard form of Crossover has 4 rows—or two loops—of beads. The first loop is the **starting loop,** and the second loop of beads crosses over the front and down the back of the starting loop. A pattern that uses Continuous Crossover Loops will look something like this:

Make 1: 7x CCL, 1 ¼ inches (3.2 cm) of beads for the starting loop.

Translation: Make one unit. The unit will have seven Continuous Crossover Loops. The **starting loop** *(the first loop that will form the base of the petals) for each petal will be made of 1 ¼ inches of beads. Notice that a measurement is not given for the second loop that crosses over the first. This is because the exact amount may vary due to individual differences in technique from one artist to another. You should use however many beads fit, though it is usually a similar length as the starting loop.*

For this exercise, use 26 or 24 gauge wire and approximately 4 grams of beads. Follow the sample pattern above. I am using a non-matching wire to make the wire paths more visible.

1. String all the seed beads onto the wire.

2. Leave a small tail wire, then form a Loop using 1 ¼ inches (3.2 cm) of beads. Twist the wires only one or two full rotations below the loop. *More twists here will leave extra wire bulk that is harder to conceal in Crossover Loops.* Mold the starting loop so it is long and thin, with only a little empty space in the middle (**Photo 1**).

3. Feed more beads from the spool and bring the wire over the front of the starting loop. Measure out the beads needed to reach the top center of the starting loop. The bottom of this row of beads should be is even with, or slightly above the bottom of the starting loop. If the beads extend below the starting loop, it will be harder to shape the finished petals, and it will be less attractive. Likewise, the top of this row of beads should be even with, or slightly below the top center of the starting loop. If they extend above the loop the wire will not be held securely between beads. (**Photo 2**)

4. Fold a bare section of wire over the top of the starting loop, making sure the wire fits snugly between two beads in the center of the loop (**Photo 3**).

5. Keep tension on the wire so it doesn't slip out of place or loosen, and so gaps don't form between the beads. Fold the wire over the back of the starting loop (**Photo 4**).

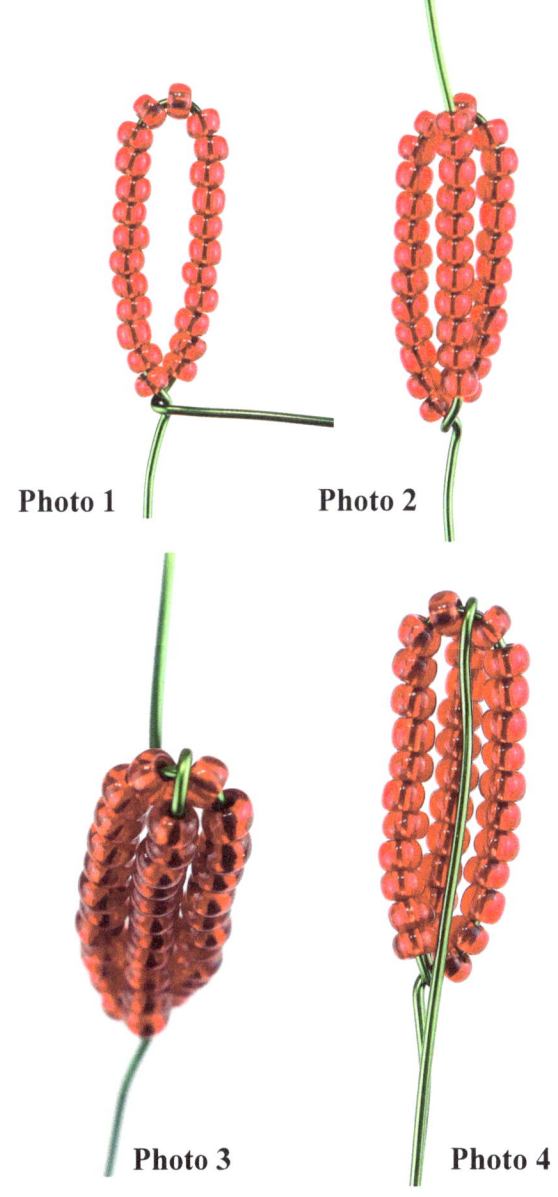

Photo 1 **Photo 2**

Photo 3 **Photo 4**

Lauren Harpster

Learn French Beading: Beginner Course

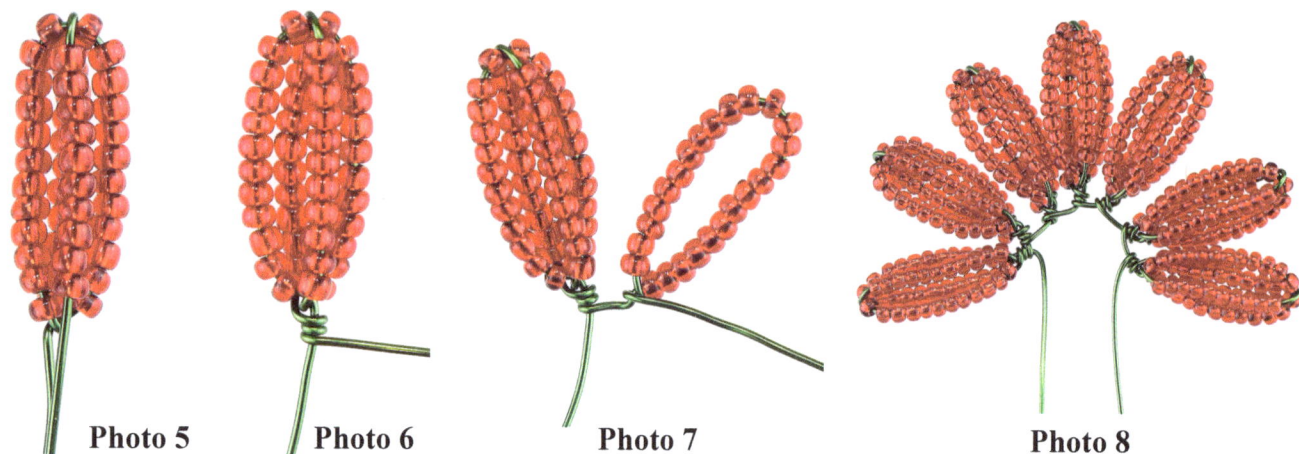

Photo 5   Photo 6   Photo 7   Photo 8

6. Feed more beads from the spool and push them all the way against the top center on the back of the starting loop. Measure out the beads needed to reach the bottom wire. They should not extend below the starting loop (**Photo 5**).

7. Tie off the working wire by wrapping it twice around the bottom wire just below the starting loop. Keep the wraps tight and close together. (**Photo 6**) *Alternatively, you could twist the two wires below two or three times.*

8. Leave a small space in the wire, then form the starting loop for the second petal using 1 ¼ inches of beads (**Photo 7**).

9. Repeat steps 3-8 until you have seven petals total (**Photo 8**).

10. The petals will look a little more cylindrical at first. Gently flatten the rows of beads in the petals so they lay side-by-side by pressing them between your thumb and forefinger.

11. Close the unit by wrapping the Working Wire around the first petal and bringing it to the underside of the petal.

*NOTE: Notice that just like with the larger CL unit from Lesson One, the two wires are off to the side of the unit (**Photo 9**), which will make it harder to center the unit on a flower stem wire.*

Photo 9

12. To center the wires, cross the working wire over the bottom of the unit and loop it around one of the petals on the opposite side. (**Photo 10**).

13. Bring the tail and working wires together in the center beneath the unit and twist them together to make the unit stem wire. (**Photo 11**)

Photo 12 shows the finished CCL unit.

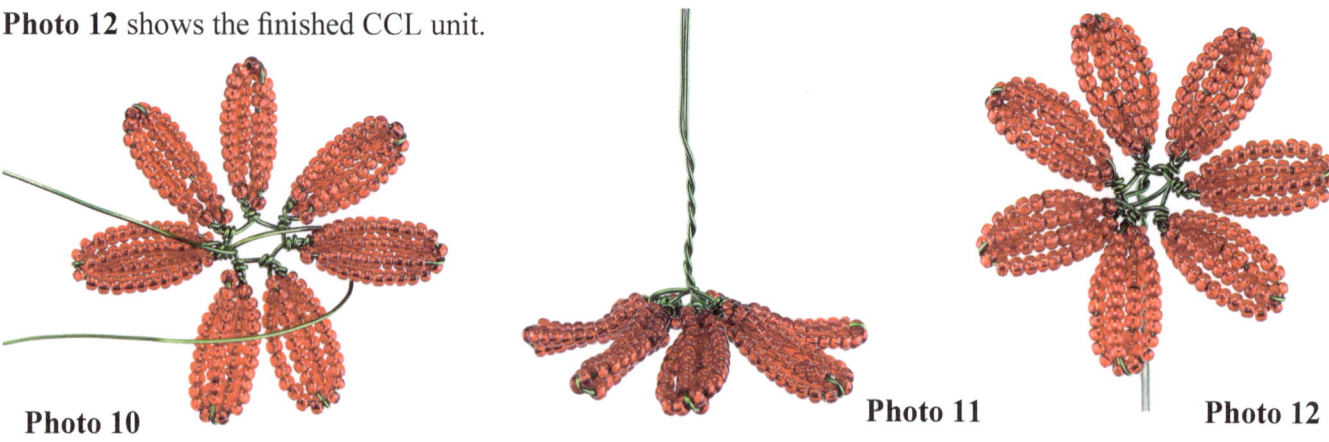

Photo 10   Photo 11   Photo 12

Lesson Three: Continuous Wraparound Loops

Terms to Remember
- Wraparound Loops
- CWL
- Bottom Wire
- Pointed Bottom (PB)
- Round Bottom (RB)

Continuous Wraparound Loops are often abbreviated in French Beading patterns as **CWL**. Like Crossover Loops, Wraparound Loops begin with a starting loop, with more loops of beads wrapped around the outside edges.

With Continuous Wraparound Loops, we start to see how to change the petal shape by wrapping at different angles. Wrapping at the **Bottom Wire** - or the wire below the loop - at a 45 degree angle will produce a **Pointed Bottom (PB)**. Wrapping at the Bottom Wire at a 90 degree angle will produce a **Round Bottom (RB)**.

Sample Pattern:
Make 1: 5x 3 row (or triple) CWL using 11 beads for the starting loop, PB.

Translation: You will make one unit. The unit will have 5 Continuous Wraparound Loop petals. Each petal will have 3 rows of beads. The starting loop for each petal should be made of 11 beads. Each petal should have a pointed bottom - wrap at a 45 degree angle.

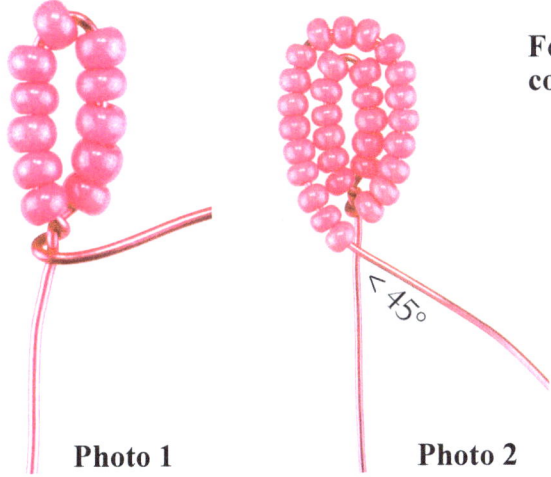

Photo 1   Photo 2

TIP: I like to rotate my petal with one hand while I wrap the row around it with the other hand, which helps fit the next row exactly around the previous one.

For this exercise use 26 or 24 gauge (0.4 - 0.5 mm) copper core wire and approximately 5 grams of size 11/0 beads.

1. String all the beads onto the wire.

2. Leave a 2 inch (5 cm) tail wire before making an 11 bead loop (**Photo 1**). Only twist below the loop one full rotation (two twists). Twisting more in CWL will leave more exposed wires between rows.

3. Feed more beads down the working wire and wrap them around the outer edge of the starting loop. Keep this row of beads directly beside the starting loop. If they are too far apart the petals will have visible gaps between rows. If they are too close, the rows of beads will bunch up on top of each other. Measure the beads needed to reach the Bottom Wire. Cross the working wire over the *front* of the Bottom Wire, creating a 45 degree angle (**Photo 2**)

4. Wrap the working wire around the bottom wire once. As you cross back over the front of the bottom wire, angle the working wire upward to complete the point and start the point of the next row (**Photo 3**).

5. Feed more beads down the Working Wire from the spool. Wrap another row of beads around the outer edge of the previous row. At the Bottom Wire, wrap at a 45 degree angle to make a Pointed Bottom. The petal now has all three rows of beads. To secure the working wire, wrap it tightly around the bottom wire below the petal twice, keeping the wraps close together. (**Photo 4**).

Photo 3   Photo 4

Lauren Harpster

Learn French Beading: Beginner Course

TIP: *Notice in Photo 5 that I've turned the second petal at a 90 degree angle from the first petal. This keeps the bottom wire for the second petal straight while wrapping on rows of beads, which makes it easier to measure out the correct amount of beads for each row and prevents a lopsided petal.*

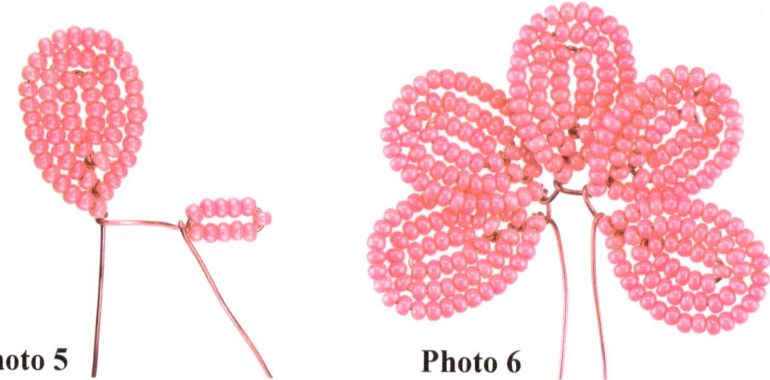

Photo 5 Photo 6

6. To begin the second petal you will need to leave a length of bare wire below the starting loop. This will be the second petal's bottom wire. The length should be the same length as the bottom wire in the first petal, plus a tiny bit extra. (**Photo 5**).

7. Repeat steps 3-6 to until you have five petals total. (**Photo 6**)

8. Close the unit the same way you would a Continuous Loop unit. Cross the working wire over the top of the first petal and wrap around it once. Then twist the wires together beneath the unit.

Photo 7 shows the finished petal unit.

Round Bottom

To make a **round bottom (RB)**, there is one simple change to the angle of the wraps. Instead of crossing over the bottom wire at a 45 degree angle, cross over at a 90 degree angle as shown in **Photo 8**.

I *personally* find that with small petals, it doesn't make a great deal of difference, so I always make mine with a pointed bottom. If you compare **Photo 9** below with the pointed petals above in **Photo 7** you'll notice that they look almost the same. But the difference does become more noticeable when making petals larger than three rows. See **Photo 10** for a shape comparison of larger CWL with a round bottom and pointed bottom.

However, since I developed the Continuous Basic Frame technique several years back, which is taught in the Intermediate Course on my website, I rarely use Continuous Wraparound Loops for anything larger than a few rows. If you do make 4+ rows, I recommend lacing them as the rows tend to separate. You can learn all about lacing in Lesson Six.

Photo 7

Photo 8

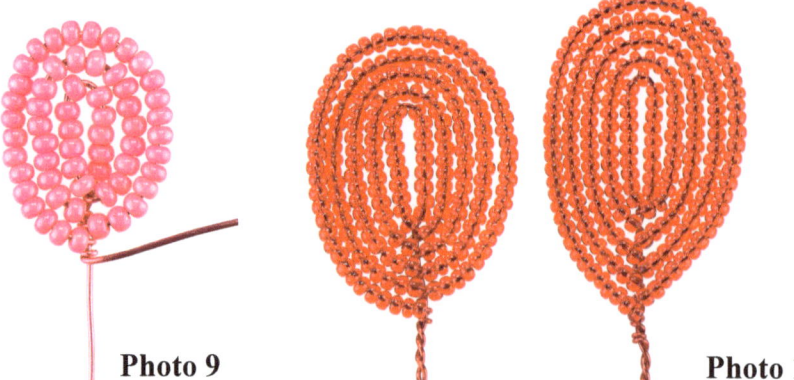

Photo 9 Photo 10

Lesson Four: Fringe

Terms to Remember
- Twisted Fringe
- Wire-Back
- Fringe Loops
- Loop Fringe
- Branching Fringe

There are two basic types of Fringes - Twisted Fringes and Wire-Back Fringes. I should note that most designers do not call them by these names. They are both generally just called Fringe, or nothing at all. These techniques are very commonly used to make flower stamen and other small pieces.

Twisted Fringe

The **Twisted Fringe** variety is very simply a bead or a loop of beads on a long twisted stem of wire. These can be continuous or single.

Sample Pattern
Make 1: 6x ½ inch (1.3 cm) Twisted Fringes with 3 beads at the tip.

Translation: Make one unit. The unit will have six Twisted Fringes. Each fringe will be ½ inch long. And there should be 3 beads at the tip of each fringe.

For this exercise, we will use 28 gauge (0.315 mm) wire because it's easier to twist. The beads are size 11/0. You will also need a ruler!

1. String 18 beads onto the 28 gauge wire. You can leave the wire attached to the spool.

2. Leave a 2 inch (5 cm) tail wire, which will be the unit stem wire after the piece is complete.

3. Measure out another 1 inch (2.5 cm) of wire. Use your fingernail to make a little notch at the beginning and end of the 1 inch section of wire. This will help match up the two sides later. Slide 3 of the beads from the spool onto this section of wire. (**Photo 1**)

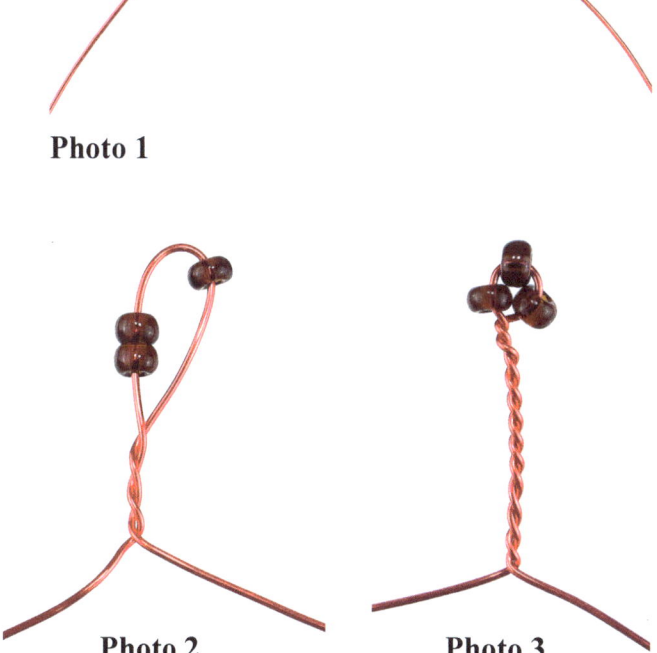

Photo 1

Photo 2   Photo 3

NOTE: *Notice that the wire we measure out is 1 inch long. When we fold it in half to twist it, the result is a ½ inch fringe. Some patterns will tell you how much wire to measure out, and others will tell you the finished length of the fringe.*

4. Fold the wire exactly in half, matching up the notches in the wire. Make sure the 3 beads are caught in the middle. Twist the two wires below, starting at the notches and moving up to the beads (**Photos 2 & 3**). This completes the first fringe.

NOTE: *Some find it easier to first cross the wires directly below the beads, then twist down to the bottom of the fringe instead of starting at the bottom. Try both to see which method suits you better.*

Lauren Harpster

Learn French Beading: Beginner Course

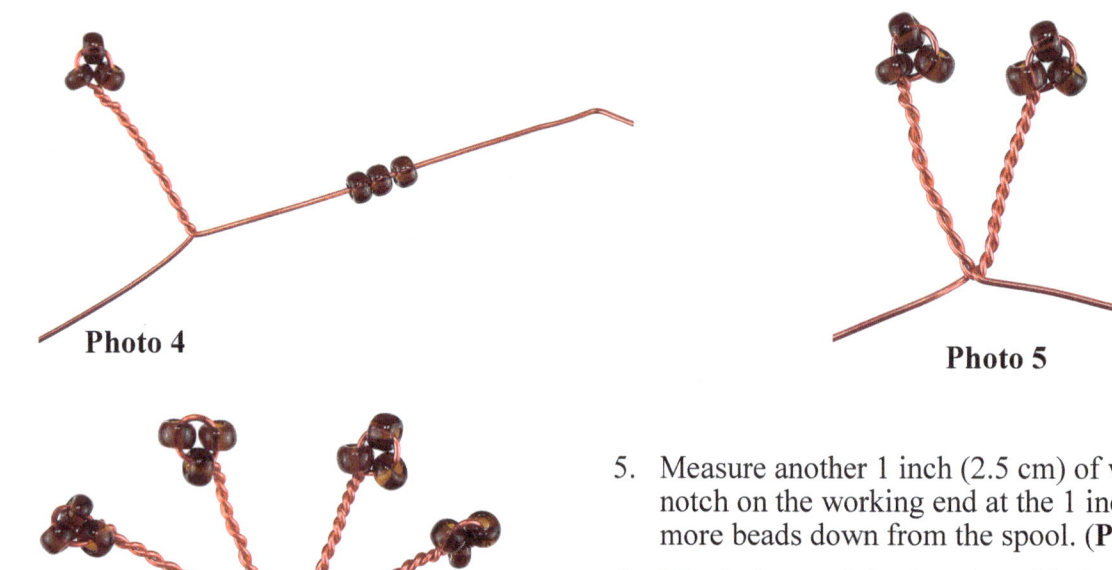

5. Measure another 1 inch (2.5 cm) of wire and make a notch on the working end at the 1 inch mark. Slide 3 more beads down from the spool. (**Photo 4**)

6. Match the notch in the wire with the base of the first fringe and make sure the 3 beads are positioned in the center. Twist the two wires below the beads together tightly against the base of the first fringe. (**Photo 5**)

7. Repeat until you have 6 total twisted fringes. (**Photo 6**)

8. Close the unit into a circle by wrapping the working wire around the first fringe once (**Photo 7**). Measure out 2 inches (5 cm) of working wire and clip from the spool.

9. Twist the tail wire and working wire together below the unit. You do not need to twist all the way down, just an inch or so. Leave the rest untwisted.

The finished unit is shown in **Photos 8 & 9.**

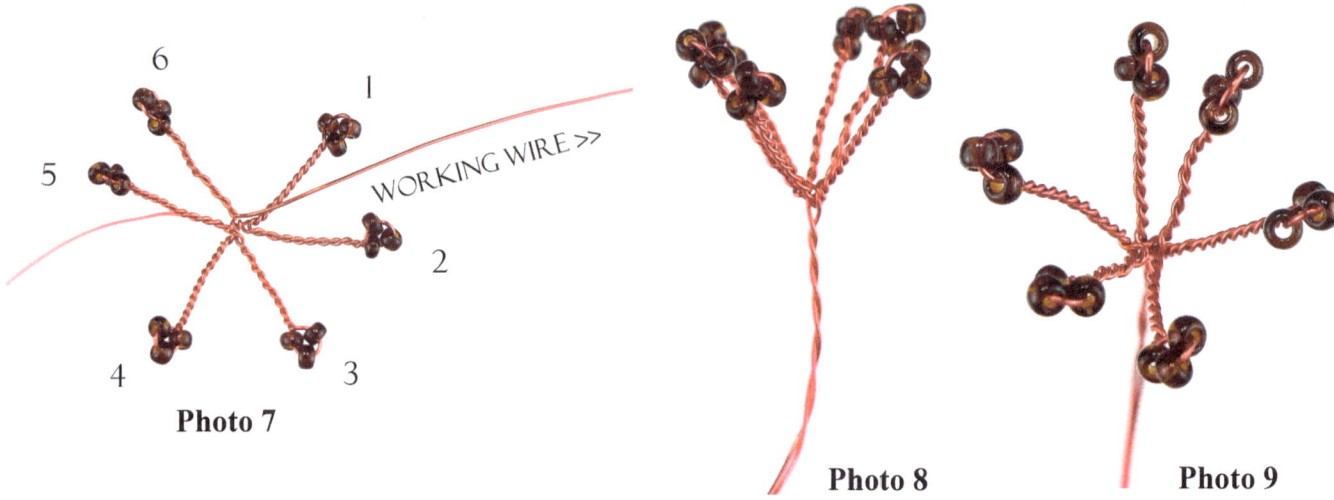

NOTE: *Just like with other continuous techniques, if the unit has a larger number of fringes, simply twisting the two wires together on the side of the unit will make it harder to center it on the flower stem wire. Center the unit stem wire by looping the working wire around one fringe on the opposite side of the unit. Then bring both wires together in the center and twist.*

Lesson Four: Fringe

Wire-Back Fringe

There is an old rule in French Beading that says the wire can only pass through the beads once to qualify as the French method. The **Wire-Back Fringe** breaks that rule, since the wire will have to pass through the beads twice. It allows you to make fringes that are made entirely of beads, instead of exposed twists of wire.

Because the wire passes through the beads twice, you will need to make sure the wire you are using will fit through the beads twice. For size 11/0 seed beads it's *usually* a 28 gauge (0.315 mm) wire.

Sample Pattern:

Make 1: 8x 10-bead Fringes
Translation: Make 1 unit. The unit will have 8 fringes. Each fringe will be 10 beads long.

For this exercise, use 28 gauge wire and < 1 gram size 11/0 seed beads.

1. Do not string any the beads on the spool of wire. Cut a 14 inch (35.6 cm) length of wire from the spool.

2. String 10 beads onto the wire and slide them down approximately 2 inches (5 cm) from one end.

3. Skipping the 10th bead, insert the working end of the wire back down through the bottom 9 beads (**Photo 10**). You should be going back down the way the wire came out. The first bead will act as a stopper at the tip of the fringe so the wire doesn't slide all the way out.

4. Hold the 9 beads in place so they don't move around on the wire. Pull the working wire all the way through to tighten the fringe. (**Photo 11**)

5. Add 10 more beads to the working wire for the second fringe. Turn them at a 90 degree angle from the first fringe. *This shortens the wire that is between the fringes to keep them close together.* Skip the top bead and insert the working wire into the 9 beads below (**Photo 12**).

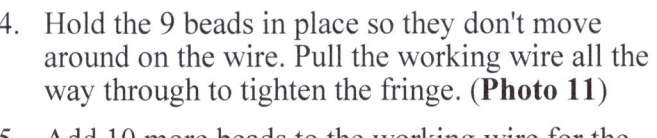

Photo 10   Photo 11

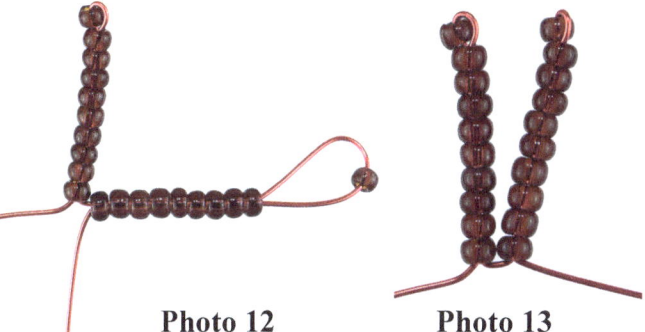

Photo 12   Photo 13

6. Pinch both the first and second fringe between your thumb and forefinger on one hand to hold them in place. Then pull the working wire through to tighten the second fringe (**Photo 13**).

7. Continue making 10 bead fringes until there are 8 total on the wire (**Photo 14**).

8. Close the unit by wrapping the working wire once around the first fringe, then center the wire below following the instructions for centering stem wires in the Continuous Loop lesson.

The finished unit is shown in **Photo 15**.

Photo 14   Photo 15

Lauren Harpster

Learn French Beading: Beginner Course

Working with Long Wire-Back Fringes

Whenever you're working with a pattern that uses Wire-Back Fringes that are really long, you may find that your working wire starts kinking more easily at the tips where you're trying to shove it through a long line of beads. In this case, I find it easier to move the beads onto the working wire, rather than trying to slide the wire through the beads. *I am demonstrating with short fringes just so all the parts will fit inside a decent sized photo.*

Before you begin, you will need to cut the wire a little longer to allow yourself a little more slack.

1. Make the first fringe by stringing all the beads for the fringe. Move the last bead out of the way, and position the working wire just above the beads in the wire-back portion of the fringe. Slide the beads up onto the working wire, and move them around until the fringe is positioned approximately 2 inches (5 cm) from one end of the wire. Pull the working wire through to tighten the fringe.

2. For all of the following fringes, add all the beads for the fringe at once. Pull the tip stopper bead out of the way and further down the working wire. Fold the working wire on itself and position the end of the wire above the beads in the wire-back portion of the fringe. (**Photo 16**)

3. Slide the beads up onto the doubled working wire. (**Photo 17**)

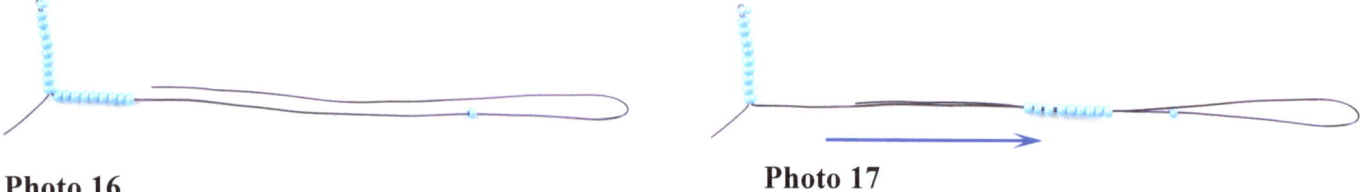

Photo 16   **Photo 17**

4. Once the beads are all the way up above the end of the working wire, pull the working wire down until it is past the first fringe. (**Photo 18**)

5. Move the beads back down into position at the bottom of the first fringe. (**Photo 19**)

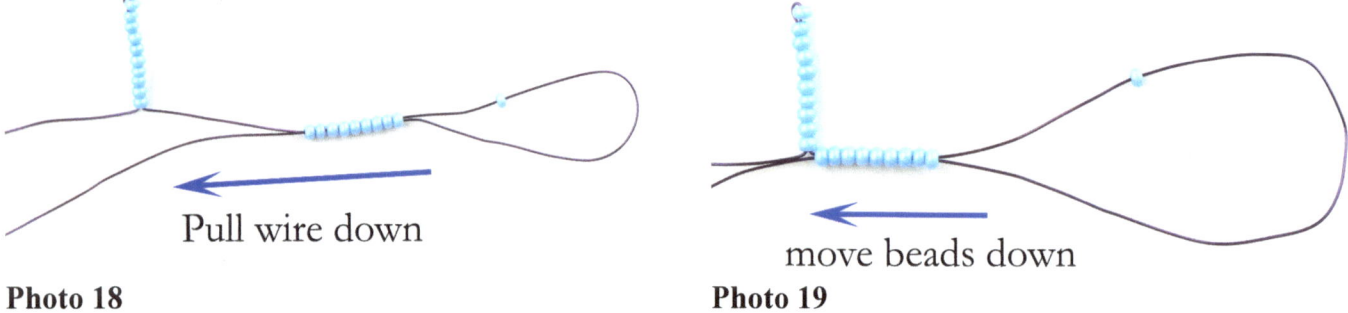

Photo 18   **Photo 19**

7. Pull the working wire all the way through to tighten the first bead that you skipped into position at the tip of the fringe. (**Photo 20**)

8. Repeat for all remaining fringes.

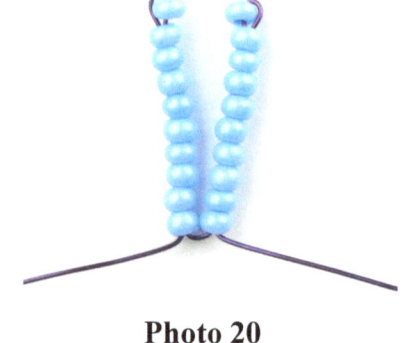

Photo 20

Lesson Four: Fringe

Next, let's take a look at some creative ways to use Wire-Back Fringes.

Loop Fringes

Loop Fringes are another great way to make a different style of stamen. You only need to make one simple alteration to a regular Wire-Back Fringe. Instead of skipping one bead at the tip of the fringe, skip as many as you want to include in the loop. I like odd numbers so a bead ends up in the middle of the loop instead of a bare spot of wire.

1. Add 22 beads to the wire.
2. Skip the last 7 beads, then wire back down through the bottom 15 beads. (**Photo 21**)
3. Repeat to make as many Loop Fringes as you'd like. (**Photo 22**)

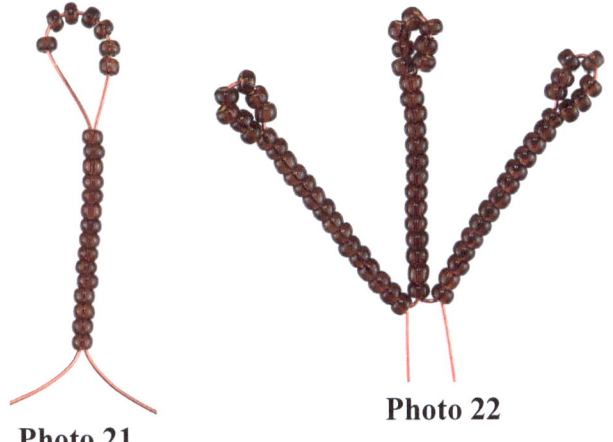

Photo 21　　**Photo 22**

Fringe Loops

This is a great way to make sepals for tiny flowers. Basically, it's the opposite of the Loop Fringes. There is fringe at the tip of a loop. The photos below show a 4 bead fringe in the middle of a 14 bead loop, which sits atop a 1-bead fringe.

1. Add 12 beads to the wire.
2. Skip the top bead and wire back through 3 beads (making a 4 bead fringe) (**Photo 23**). You will have 8 beads left on the tail wire.
3. Add 7 beads to the working end of the wire to make the second half of the loop.
4. Insert the end of the working wire into the bottom bead on the first half of the loop to make a 1-bead wire-back fringe at the bottom of the loop. (**Photo 24**)
5. Pull tight to finish the Fringe Loop. (**Photo 25**)

Alternatively, you can leave off the 1-bead wire-back at the bottom and just twist the two wires together below (**Photo 26**)

Photo 23　　**Photo 24**

Photo 25　　**Photo 26**

Lauren Harpster

Branching Fringe

Yet another way to use wire-back fringes is to make one fringe inside of another fringe to make branching fringes.

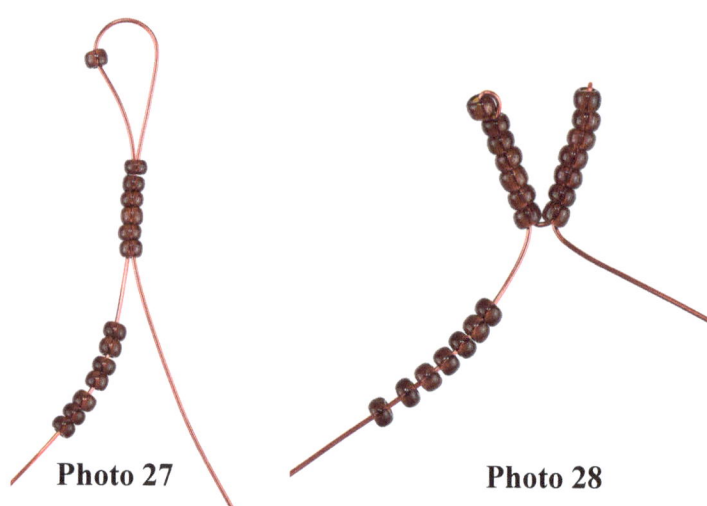

Photo 27   **Photo 28**

1. Measure and cut about 10 inches (25.4 cm) of bare wire from the spool.

2. String 14 beads onto the wire. Skip the top bead and wire-back through 6 beads below (**Photo 27**). There will be 7 beads left on the tail wire. Leave them alone for now, but make a loop in the end of your tail wire so they don't fall off.

3. Add 7 more beads to the working wire and make a second fringe beside the first one (**Photo 28**).

4. Wire-back through the 7 beads that were leftover in step 2 (**Photo 29**). You will end up with a Y-shaped fringe.

5. Add 14 more beads to the working wire to start the second Y. Complete the first 7 bead fringe by skipping the first bead and wiring back through 6 beads. You will need to keep this second Y very close to the first Y to prevent gaps in the wire between them (**Photo 30**).

Photo 29 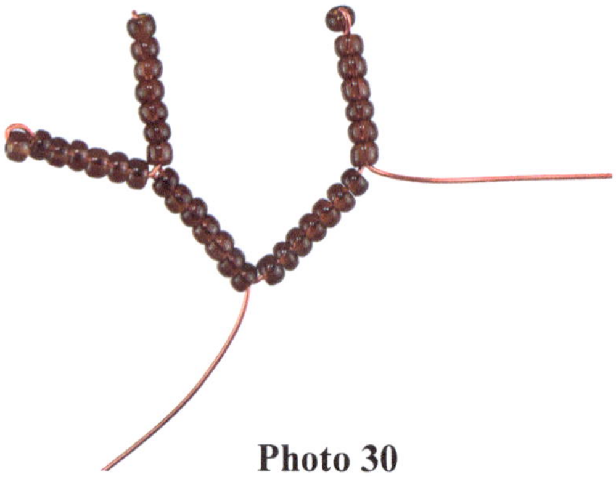   **Photo 30** 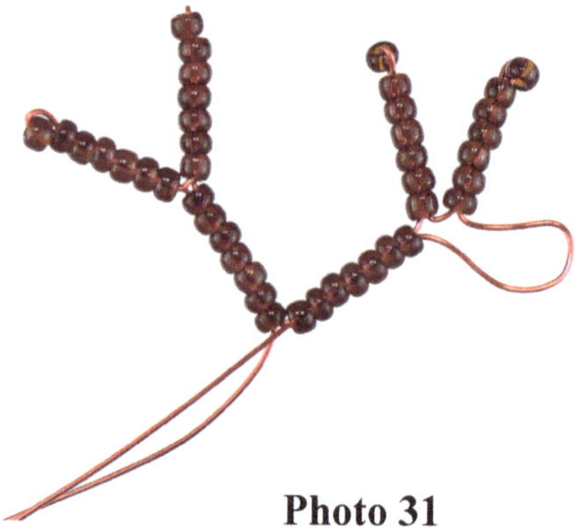   **Photo 31**

Photo 32

6. Add 7 beads to the working wire. Skip the first bead and wire back through 6 beads to make the second fringe in the second Y.

7. Wire back through the 7 beads below to complete the second Y (**Photos 31 & 32**).

Lesson Five: Basic Frame

Terms to Remember
- Basic Frame (BF)
- Top Wire
- Bottom Wire
- Basic Row (BR)
- Bottom Loop
- Working Wire
- Round Bottom (RB)
- Pointed Bottom (PB)
- Round Top (RT)
- Pointed Top (PT)
- One Bottom Wire
- Two Bottom Wires
- Three Bottom Wires
- Reverse Wrap (RW)

Basic Frame (sometimes abbreviated as **BF**) is the most commonly used French Beading technique.

A Basic Frame petal begins with a **Basic Row (or BR)** in the center of the leaf or petal. When counting rows, the Basic Row is row number 1. All of the other rows are wrapped around the Basic Row along two axis wires: the Top Wire (also called the Basic Wire) - which is above the Basic Row - and the Bottom Wire - which is below the Basic Row. Each pass over either axis counts as another row.

Photo 1 shows the four basic shapes that can be created on a Basic Frame. These leaves were all made with a 9 row Basic Frame, 10 bead Basic Row, changing only the angle of the wraps to make different shapes. In patterns that are written in shorthand, these shapes will be designated by the letters "P" for pointed, or "R" for round. This letter will be paired with either a "B" for bottom, or "T" for top, which tells you which end to make in that shape.

RB PT   PB PT   RB RT   PB RT

- To make a **Pointed Top (PT)**, wrap at the Top Wire at a 45 degree angle.
- To make a **Round Top (RT)**, wrap at the Top Wire at a 90 degree angle.
- To make a **Pointed Bottom (PB)**, wrap at the Bottom Wire at a 45 degree angle.
- To make a **Round Bottom (RB)**, wrap at the Bottom Wire at a 90 degree angle.

Photo 1

Sample Pattern:
Make 1: 9 row BF, 10 bead BR, PT RB.
- **Reduce to two bottom wires.**

Translation: Make one leaf. Use the Basic Frame technique with 9 rows total. The Basic Row (row #1) will be 10 beads long. The leaf will have a Pointed Top (45 degree angle) and a Round Bottom (90 degree angle). After finishing the rows of beads on the leaf, reduce the number of Bottom Wires to two.

For this exercise, use 24 gauge (0.5 mm) copper core wire and a few grams of size 11/0 seed beads. Follow the sample pattern above.

1. String all of the beads onto the spool of wire, then make a small loop in the end of the wire. This acts as a stopper to prevent the beads from sliding off.
2. Count out 10 beads for the Basic Row from the spool and slide them toward the end of the wire. Leave a small length of wire above. This will be the Top Wire (also called the Basic Wire).
3. Make a loop in the wire below the Basic Row by crossing the wire over itself directly below the Basic Row (**Photo 2**).

Photo 2

Lauren Harpster

Learn French Beading: Beginner Course

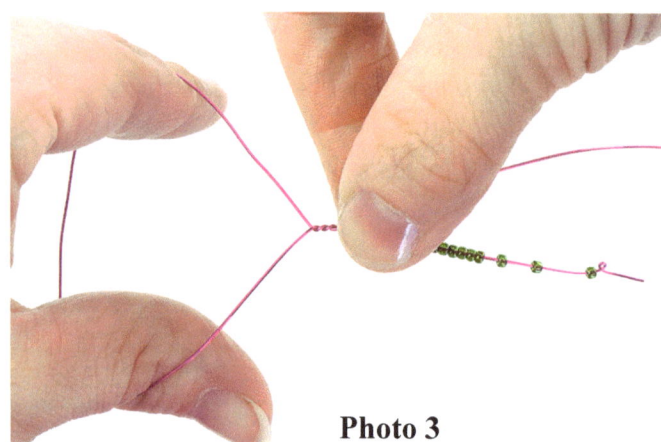

Photo 3

4. To complete the frame, pinch and hold right where the two wires cross with one hand, then twist the loop below with the other hand. (**Photo 3**)

TIP: *Keep the twists in these wires nice and smooth. To do this, use your forefinger and thumb to open up the bottom loop in a v-shape. Make sure the two wires that make up the loop are at the same angle from where the twisted wire forms. Pull down on these wires with equal pressure while you twist.*

Photo 4 shows the finished Basic Frame. Take note of the "anatomy".

- In the center is a row of 10 beads. This is the Basic Row, or row number 1.
- Above the Basic Row is the Top Wire.
- Right below the Basic Row is the Working Wire. This should still be attached to the spool and strung with beads.
- Below the Working Wire is a twisted double wire which is the Bottom Wire. This will become the leaf's stem wire which will attach it to the flower stem.
- Below the Bottom Wire is the Loop, which will also be part of the leaf's unit stem wire.

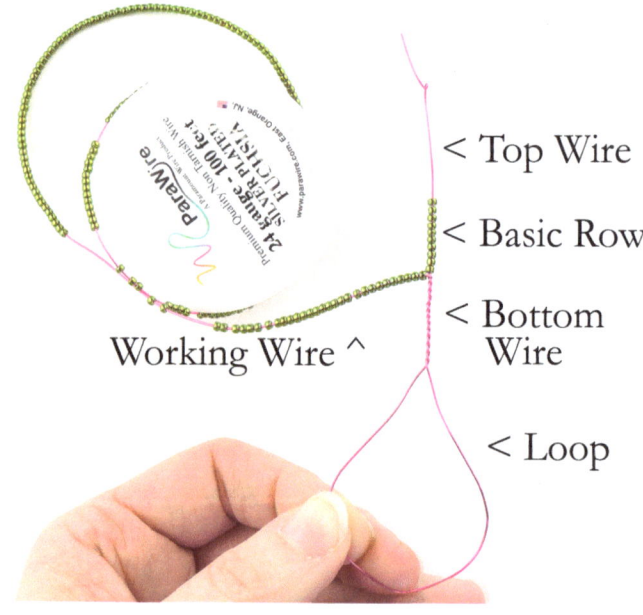

Photo 4

5. Feed more beads down the Working Wire until they are flush against the frame. Fold the beads up *directly* beside the Basic Row toward the Top Wire.

6. Measure the beads needed to reach the Top Wire. The pattern tells us to make a Pointed Top. Cross the Working Wire *over the front* of the Top Wire, making a 45 degree angle with the Top Wire (**Photo 5**).

7. Wrap around the Top Wire. As you bring the Working Wire back to the front of the leaf, angle it down, making another 45 degree angle with the Basic Row (**Photo 6**). This completes row 2.

8. Feed more beads down the Working Wire and lay them flat against the other side of the Basic Row, pointing toward the Bottom Wire.

Photo 5   Photo 6

Lesson Five: Basic Frame

TIP: *I rotate my piece while I'm wrapping rows so I am always working at the top, which is why Photos 7 and 8 are up-side down. I find it is much easier to wrap this way.*

Photo 7   Photo 8

9. Measure the beads needed to reach the Bottom Wire. The pattern tells us to make a Round Bottom. Cross the Working Wire *over the front* of the Bottom Wire, making a 90 degree angle (**Photo 7**).

10. Wrap around the Bottom Wire, maintaining a 90 degree angle as the Working Wire crosses back over the front (**Photo 8**). The leaf now has 3 rows of beads.

11. Continue wrapping rows until you have 9 total, or 4 rows on each side of the Basic Row (**Photo 9**). Remember to wrap at a 45 degree angle at the Top Wire, and a 90 degree at the Bottom Wire. Make certain to keep track of which side of the petal is the front, and which is the back. The wire wraps and the top and bottom wires should only show on the back side.

NOTE: *It is important to keep the Top and Bottom Wires of the frame straight while you wrap rows. If you allow the wires to bend, the leaf will end up lop-sided. If they do bend out of place, gently pull the Top and Bottom Wires in opposite directions at the same time to straighten them.*

12. After completing the required number of rows, "tie off" the Working Wire by wrapping it twice below the last row on the Bottom Wire. These wraps should be tight and close together. (**Photo 10**)

Photo 9

Photo 10

13. The pattern says to "reduce to two Bottom Wires". To do this, simply use some wire cutters to carefully remove the Working Wire. Clip it very close to the Bottom Wire (**Photo 11**).

14. Twist the two remaining Bottom Wires together approximately 1 inch (2.5 cm) below the leaf. Leave the rest untwisted. Cut the bottom loop open and trim the wires to different lengths - *this will help keep the flower stem tidy during assembly*. Cut the Top Wire short, approximately ¼ inch (6 mm) (**Photo 12**). Then fold it down against the back of the leaf.

Note: *As you twist the bottom wires down, try to keep the twists smooth, just like when you constructed the frame. Any lumps in the petal or leaf stem wires will make lumps on the finished flower stem.*

Photo 11   Photo 12

Learn French Beading: Beginner Course

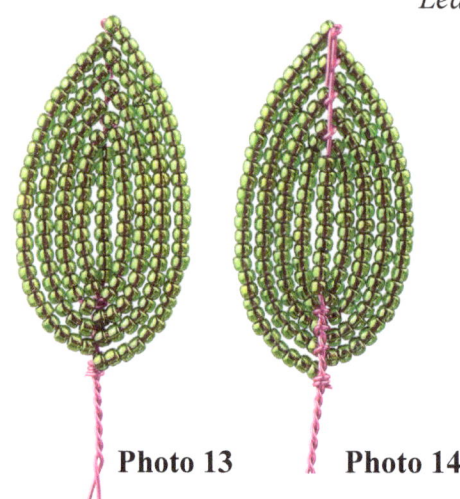

Photo 13   Photo 14

The front of the finished leaf is shown in **Photo 13**. The back of the leaf is shown in **Photo 14**. Notice that the top and bottom wires, along with all the wire wraps, are only visible on the back of the leaf.

Different sizes of petals and leaves require a different amount of support to prevent them from drooping. Reducing the number of stem wires when you can helps keep the flower stem thin.

- **Reduce to 1 Bottom Wire**- Only do this for very small parts that don't need a great deal of support. To do this, remove the working wire, then separate the wires in the loop and carefully cut one of them just below the wraps in the working wire "tie off". I do not recommend reducing to 1 bottom wire for pieces with just 3 rows. There are not enough twists between the bottom of the basic row and the bottom of the petal to hold it together. A leaf with 1 bottom wire is shown in **Photo 15**.

- **Reduce to 2 Bottom Wires** - for small or medium pieces. This is shown in the Basic Frame technique instructions on page 34.

- **3 Bottom Wires** - Heavier medium to large sized pieces will need 3 bottom wires to prevent them from drooping. Just like constructing the initial frame, we want to keep this wire as smooth as possible to prevent lumps on the flower stem. Untwist any sections of the bottom wire that are twisted, and straighten them as best you can. Then line the working wire up in between the two bottom wires, and pull down while twisting them together. A leaf with 3 bottom wires is shown in **Photos 16 & 17**.

Photo 15

Photo 16   Photo 17

Photo 18   Photo 19

Reverse Wrap

A Reverse Wrap is a simple modification of the Basic Frame where you wrap around one of the frame wires by crossing over the *back* of the wire, while wrapping the other frame wire over the normally by crossing over the front of the wire. This will make the wire wraps exposed on opposite sides of the petal. Look at **Photos 18 and 19**. They show two sides of the same leaf. On one side, the wires are exposed on the top. On the other side, the wires are exposed on the bottom. This technique helps conceal frame wires when both sides of the petal would be visible in the finished flower. This may sometimes be abbreviated in patterns as **RW**.

Lesson Six: Lacing

Terms to Remember
- Lacing
- Lace-as-you-go

Simply put, lacing is sewing across a petal or leaf with a thin gauge of wire. **Photo 1** shows a petal that is unlaced. Even if your technique is perfect the rows of beads in petals over a certain size will separate, leaving the petal looking unkempt. Shaping the petal into a more natural shape with bends and twists and folds creates a disastrous mess. We fix this problem with **Lacing**.

Lacing is used to prepare our flower components for assembly. It's one of the things that many French Beaded Flower artists love to hate, and hate to love. Why? Because it can be a real pain in the fingers. However, it vastly improves the appearance of flowers by keeping the rows nice and tidy, and by allowing you to shape flower components into more natural shapes without getting a mess of beads and wire. Don't skip the lacing!

Not everything needs to be laced. Each artist has their own set of rules for when to lace. These are mine:

- Lace anything that is 11+ rows wide. (You don't always have to lace at 11 rows, so decide those on a case-by-case basis.)
- Lace anything that is over 2 inches (5 cm) long, no matter how many rows.
- Lace any piece that will endure a *large* amount of shaping (bending and molding pieces into natural shapes).
- For long petals and leaves, lace once for every 1 to 1 ½ inches (2.5 - 3.8 cm) along the Basic Row.
- Lace whenever YOU feel it's necessary, even if a pattern doesn't call for it!

Photo 1

For this exercise, make a Basic Frame leaf with 24 gauge (.5 mm) wire in any shape and with any size basic row that is at least 13 rows wide. Use 30-32 gauge (0.2 - 0.25 mm) copper core wire to lace. I recommend using a color of wire that closely matches the beads, if you can find it. I will be using a mismatched color so you can see it more easily in pictures.

1. To begin, cut a length of 30-32 gauge wire that is approximately 2 ½ times the width of the leaf. Fold the wire in half.
2. Insert the wire into the *front* of the petal, with one wire end on each side of the Basic Row (**Photo 2**).
3. Pull both wire ends all the way through to the back of the petal. (**Photo 3**). The center fold in the lacing wire should "catch" between two beads on the Basic Row.
4. Cross the wires on the back of the petal so they switch places (**Photo 4**).

Photo 2

Photo 3

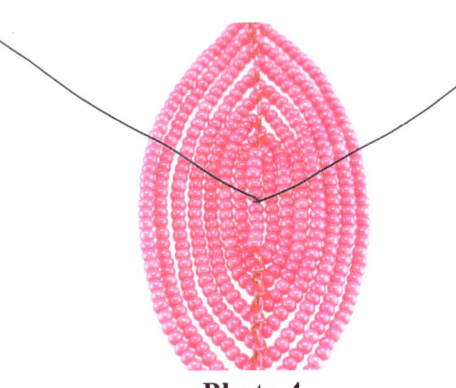

Photo 4

Lauren Harpster

Learn French Beading: Beginner Course

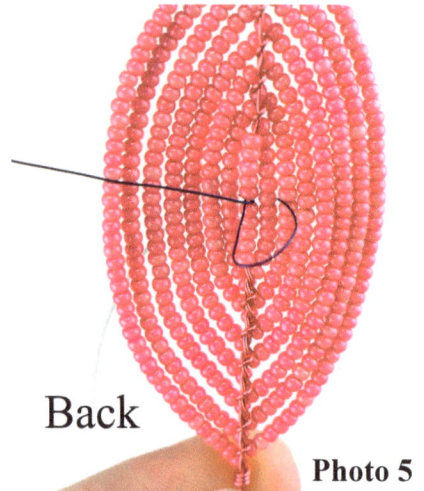
Back Photo 5

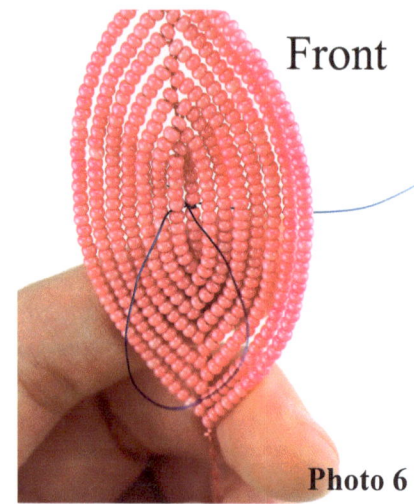
Front Photo 6

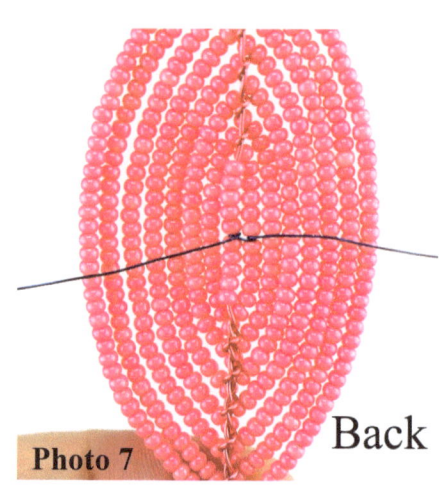
Photo 7 Back

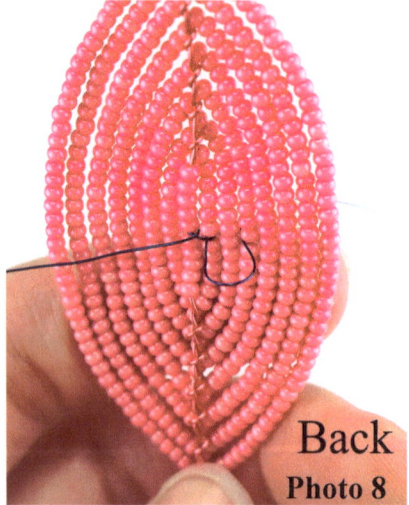
Back Photo 8

5. Still looking at the back of the petal, select one of the wire ends and insert it between the first and second rows of beads (**Photo 5**). Pull the wire all the way through to the front of the petal.

6. Flip to look at the front of the petal. Insert the end of the wire between the Basic row and the first row beside it (**Photo 6**). Pull the wire all the way through to the back, making a complete loop around the first row of beads beside the Basic Row (**Photo 7**). *If you are familiar with sewing or embroidery, this is very similar to back-stitch.* Check the front of the leaf to make sure the wire is tightly between two beads. On the front side, you shouldn't see much wire - just an almost imperceptible loop around the row. On the back there will be a wire crossing over between the Basic Row and the row beside it.

7. Repeat, skipping over a row with every loop of the lacing wire until all the rows are sewn together. If you've done it correctly, the lacing wire should only show on the back of the petal. (**Photo 8**)

TIP: *I find it very helpful to use my thumbnail to mark the petal just below the lacing line. Not only does this pinch and hold the rows together while you lace, but it also helps guide the lacing wire between the correct beads* (**Photo 9**).

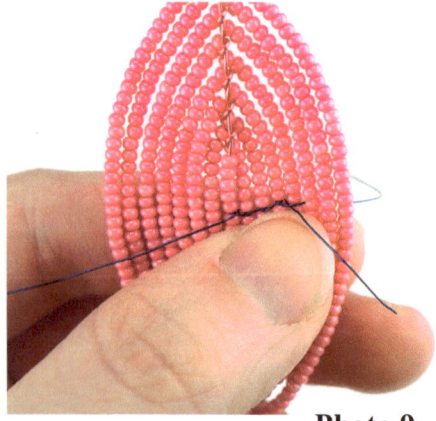
Photo 9

8. When you reach the outer edge of the petal, wrap the lacing wire twice around the last row of beads to secure it (**Photo 10**). Use wire cutters to clip it close against the petal. If there is a tiny tail of wire left, fold it down between the beads with pliers or a fingernail.

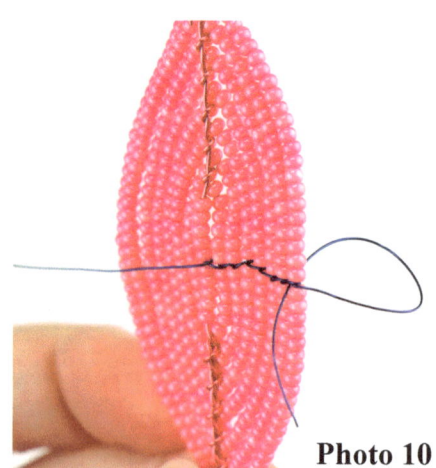
Photo 10

Lesson Six: Lacing

9. Repeat with the other wire end to lace the other half of the petal. **(Photo 11)** *I tend to flip my petal upside-down to lace the second side because it is easier for me if I move right-to-left.*

Photo 12 shows the back of the finished petal. The lacing wire should only show on the back.

Notice in **Photo 13** that rows still stay mostly together when you twist and shape the petals.

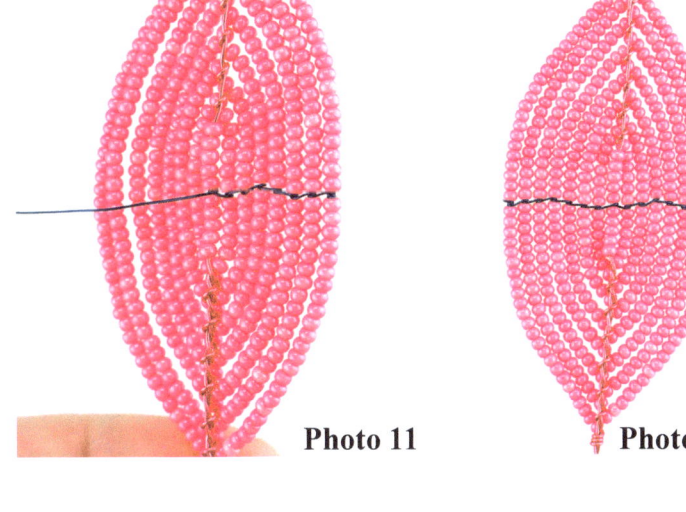

Photo 11   Photo 12

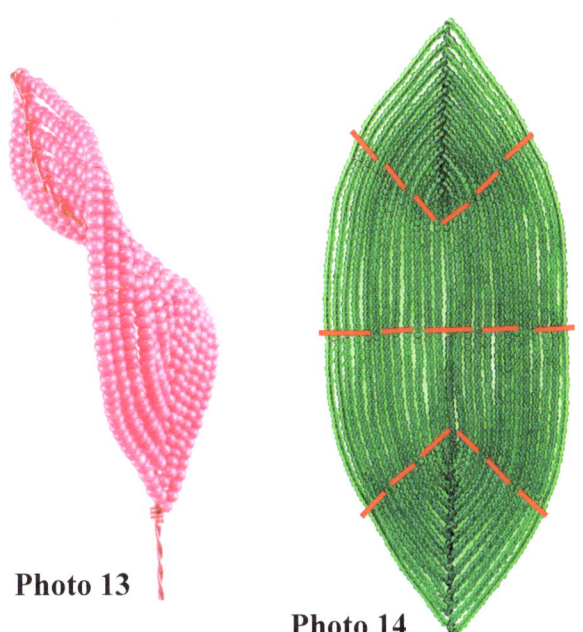

Photo 13

Photo 14

Most of the time you will lace straight across a petal or leaf. Beads won't always line up exactly to get a perfectly straight line across, but do try to get it as straight as you can.

Other times you may need to lace in a **v-shape**, especially near the top or bottom tips of a leaf. This is done exactly the same way as regular lacing, just lace at an angle rather than straight across. **Photo 14** shows an example of a leaf with a v-shaped lacing line. Sometimes my patterns will have dashed lines like these to tell you where to place the lacing wires.

NOTE: *You can also lace from one side of the leaf to the other side, instead of starting in the middle. However, because my hands are small, I find it harder to hold the piece and all the rows in place while lacing that way.*

Lace-As-You-Go

When making very long or very wide petals and leaves, it can be difficult to get the rows of beads to line up nicely. For these pieces, it is very helpful to lace them while you make them, rather than waiting until you have all the rows finished. Lacing during construction is called **Lace-as-you-go**. Some French Beading artists choose to lace all of their pieces this way, no matter the size.

1. Wrap the first three rows of a leaf. Then add in the lacing wire(s) exactly as you would with regular lacing. Lace all the rows you already have (**Photo 15**). Because this is a long leaf, it requires three lacing wires.

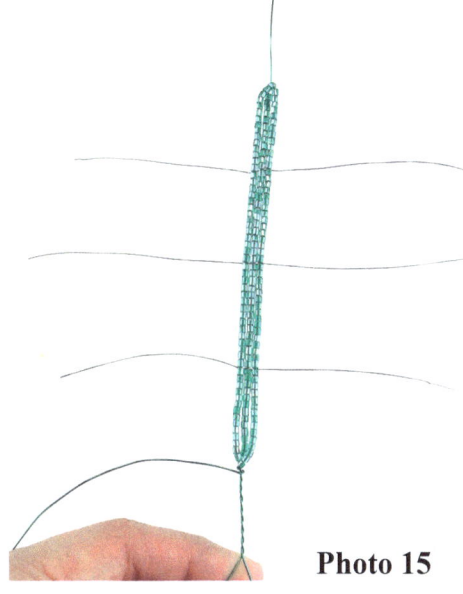

Photo 15

Lauren Harpster

Photo 16 **Photo 17** **Photo 18**

2. After the lacing wires are in place you can continue adding rows. Measure the beads needed to reach the first lacing wire, hold tension on the beads so no gaps form between them, and loop the lacing wire around. (**Photo 16**)

3. Measure the beads needed to reach the next lacing wire, hold tension, and loop the lacing wire around (**Photo 17**).

4. Repeat until you reach the end of the row, then wrap the working wire around the top or bottom wire to secure the row. (**Photo 18**)

5. Repeat on all the remaining rows.

For shorter pieces that you need to lace-as-you-go, you can carefully measure out the beads needed for the full row and wrap at the Top or Bottom Wire, then go back through and loop all the lacing wires around it before moving on to the next row.

Part 3

Practice Flower Patterns

Lavender

Flower Head Size:
Approximately 4 ¼ inches (10.8 cm) tall

Techniques Required:
- Continuous Loops

Lavender

This pattern and the materials listed below will make one stem of Bud or Blooming Lavender. For my arrangement I made four stems of Bud Lavender and three stems of Blooming Lavender.

MATERIALS:	BUD LAVENDER	BLOOMING LAVENDER
BEADS		
- 11/0 transparent AB lilac seed beads (Color A)	5 grams	5 grams
- 11/0 opal lavender seed beads (Color B)	0	4 grams
- 11/0 transparent lime green seed beads (Color C)	4 grams	4 grams
WIRE		
26 gauge (.4 mm) light purple copper core wire	8 ft (2.4 m)	15 ft (4.6 m)
26 gauge (.4 mm) lime green copper core wire	5 ft (1.5 m)	5 ft (1.5 m)
16 gauge (1.2 mm) florist stem wire	1 piece	1 piece
OTHER		
Light green floral tape	< 1 roll	< 1 roll
Light green embroidery floss (try to match the light green beads)	~ 2 yards (1.8 m)	~ 2 yards (1.8 m)

NOTE: *For the blooming lavender, I used a semi-transparent opal lavender bead for the florets, and a transparent rainbow bead for the buds. I picked a lighter color for the little florets so they will stand out more from the bud loops behind them.*

PREP:

Usually in French Beading you do not pre-string the beads when there are multiple colors used on a single unit, but with Continuous Loops you sometimes can. For something simple like the Bud Lavender, I do recommend pre-stringing the beads to make the process a little faster, and so you can work from the spool without cutting any wire.

Bud Lavender Stringing Instructions:

Pre-string beads onto the 26g (.4 mm) light purple wire in this order: 1C, 9A, 2C, 9A, 2C... until there are 54 purple sections. After the last purple section, string 1C. These strung beads will make all of the Tip Units and Bud Units for one full Bud Lavender stem.

Blooming Lavender Stringing Instructions:

The blooming components of the Blooming Lavender are harder to pre-string beads for, so we will cut wire and string beads as needed for those parts. To keep things simple we will only pre-string the beads for the components which are the same as the Bud Lavender.

Pre-string beads onto the 26g (.4 mm) light purple wire in the same order as the Bud Lavender, but only until there are 24 purple sections. After the last purple section, string 1C. These strung beads will make the Tip and Bud Units required for one Blooming Lavender.

Learn French Beading: Beginner Course

Stem Tip Unit:

Wire: 26 gauge (.4 mm) light purple
Bead Colors: A (lilac), C (lime green)

Bud Lavender: Make 1
Blooming Lavender: Make 1

Pattern: 4x 11 bead CL (1C, 9A, 1C)

Translation: Use the Continuous Loop technique to make four loops with eleven beads each. Beads for each loop should be strung in this order: 1 lime green (C), 9 lilac (A), 1 lime green (C).

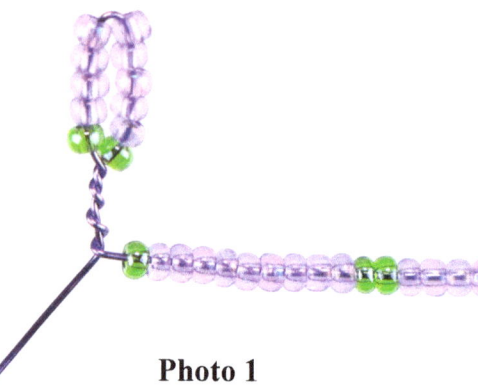

Photo 1

Instructions:

1. Work from the pre-strung spool of wire. Leave a 1-2 inch (2.5 - 5 cm) tail, then make the first loop with 11 beads (1C, 9A, 1C). Twist down approximately ¼ inch (6.4 mm) below the loop. (**Photo 1**)

2. Directly below the last twist, make 3x CL using the same bead pattern as the first, but just twisting two full rotations for each as you normally would with CL. (**Photo 2**)

3. Wrap loops 2-4 around the starting wire to position the first loop in the center. Close loops 2-4 into a circle by wrapping the working wire once around the second loop. (**Photo 3**)

4. Twist the working and tail wires together a few times below the unit. Leave the rest of the wire lengths untwisted.

5. Conceal the twisted stem below the first loop by folding the lower three loops up around it.

The finished Stem Tip Unit is shown in **Photo 4**.

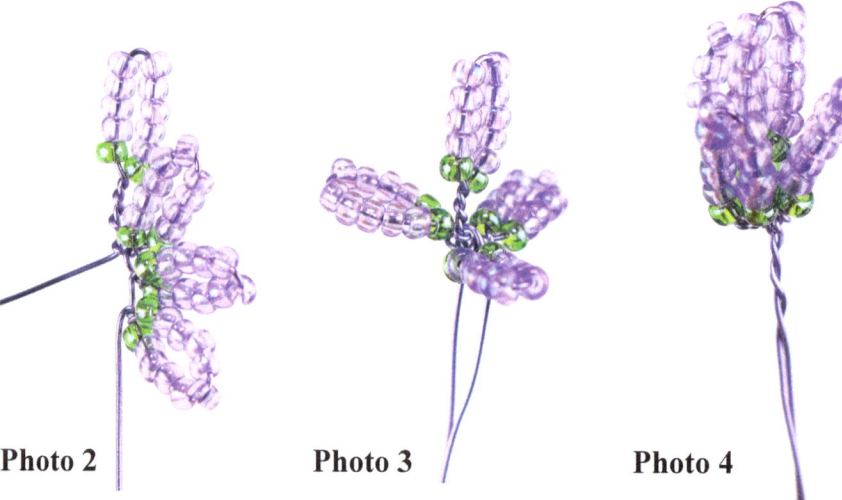

Photo 2   **Photo 3**   **Photo 4**

Bud Unit:

Wire: 26 gauge (.4 mm) light purple
Bead Colors: A (lilac), C (lime green)

Bud Lavender: Make 10
Blooming Lavender: Make 4

Pattern: 5x 11 bead CL (1C, 9A, 1C)

Translation: Use the Continuous Loop technique to make five loops with eleven beads each. Beads for each loop should be strung in this order: 1 lime green, 9 lilac, 1 lime green.

Instructions:

1. Work from the pre-strung spool. Leave a 1-2 inch (2.5 - 5 cm) tail, then make 5 loops using 1C, 9A, 1C beads each. (**Photo 5**)

2. Cut the working wire to approximately 1 inch (2.5 cm) and leave the unit open. It will make assembly easier.

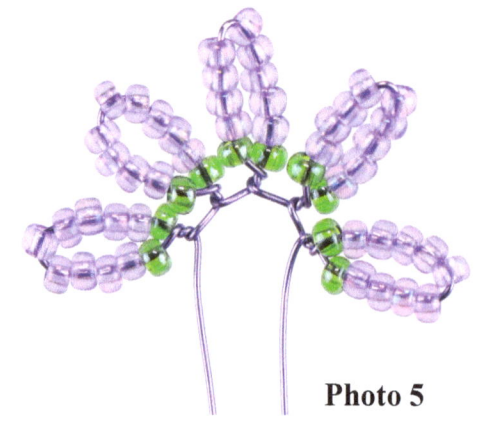

Photo 5

Lavender

Bloom Units:
Wire: 26 gauge (.4 mm) light purple
Bead Colors: A (lilac), B (lavender), C (lime green)

2-Bloom Units:
Bud Lavender: Make 0
Blooming Lavender: Make 3

Pattern: 5x loops using the patterns below. Make the loops in any order.
> 3x Bud Loops: 11 bead CL (1C, 9A, 1C)
> 2x Bloom Loops: 10 bead CL with 4x 5 bead CL in the middle (1C, 4A, 21B, 4A, 1C)

Translation: Use the Continuous Loop technique to make five total loops. Switch up the order of the loops. Three of the loops are simple Continuous Loops with 11 beads each strung in this order: 1 lime green, 9 lilac, 1 lime green. The other two loops are more complicated. Each ten-bead loop will have a cluster of four five-bead loops in the middle. For a Bloom Loop, string beads in this order: 1 lime green, 4 lilac, 21 lavender, 4 lilac, 1 lime green.

Photo 6

Instructions:

1. Cut approximately 1 ½ feet (46 cm) of wire. Make a little loop in one end of the wire to prevent beads from falling off. String 1C, 4A, 21B, 4A, 1C and slide them down toward the knotted end of the wire. Leave a 2 inch (5 cm) tail wire in front of the beads.

2. Skip the first 5 beads (1C, 4A), then make 4x 5-bead CL using the B beads (**Photo 6**). These tiny loops should be made very tight and as close together as you can manage. I only twisted my loops once full rotation so less wire would show in the finished floret.

Photo 7

3. There should be 1B left on the working end of the wire. Bring the working wire over the first 5-bead loop, and slide the last B bead into position in the center of the floret. (**Photo 7**)

4. Wrap the working wire once around the base of the first loop to secure the floret, then bring it to the underside of the flower. Twist the working wire and tail wire together once just below the flower. (**Photo 8**)

5. Slide the 4A and 1C on each of the two wires up below the flower, then tightly twist the working and tail wires below the two rows of beads. (**Photo 9**) This makes one Bloom Loop.

6. Add 1C, 9A, 1C to the working end of the wire and twist them into a Bud Loop. (**Photo 10**)

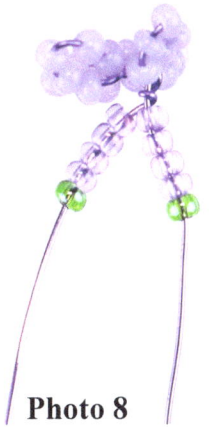

Photo 8

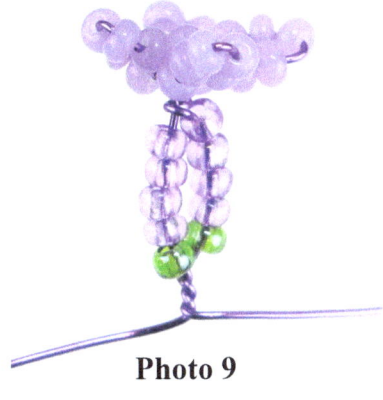

Photo 9

Photo 10

Lauren Harpster

Learn French Beading: Beginner Course

7. Add 1C, 4A, 21B, 4A, 1C to the working end of the wire.

8. Leave the same small space between the last loop and the new Bloom Loop, then repeat steps 2-5 on the previous page to make a second Bloom Loop. (**Photos 11 and 12**)

9. Add beads for two more Bud Loops to the working end of the wire, then make them into two loops. Do not close the unit. Leaving it open will make assembly easier.

The finished 2-Bloom Unit is shown in **Photo 13**.

For the remaining two 2-Bloom Units you can make the Bud and Bloom Loops in any order, or just repeat this one if you prefer.

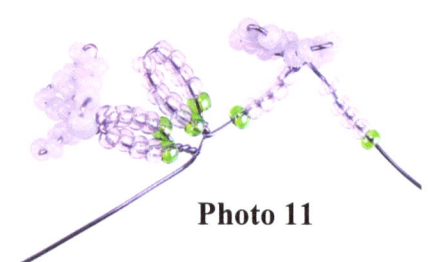
Photo 11

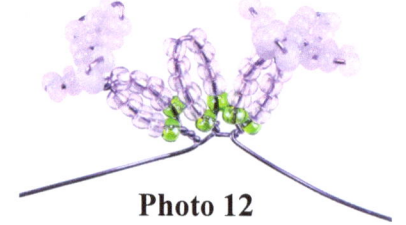
Photo 12

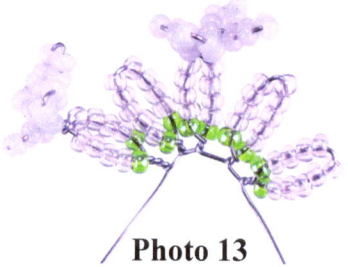
Photo 13

Photo 14

3-Bloom Units:
Bud Lavender: Make 0
Blooming Lavender: Make 3

Pattern: 5x loops using the patterns below. Make the loops in any order.
2x Bud Loops: 11 bead CL (1C, 9A, 1C)
3x Bloom Loops: 10 bead CL with 4x 5 bead CL at the tip (1C, 4A, 21B, 4A, 1C)

Translation: Use the Continuous Loop technique to make five total loops. Switch up the order of the loops. Three of the loops are simple Continuous Loops with 11 beads each strung in this order: 1 green, 9 lilac, 1 green. The other two loops are more complicated. Each ten-bead loop will have a cluster of four five-bead loops in the center. String beads in this order: 1 lime green, 4 lilac, 21 lavender, 4 lilac, 1 lime green.

Instructions:

1. Cut approximately 2 feet (61 cm) of wire from the spool.

2. Follow the same basic procedure as the 2-Bloom Units above, but make three Bloom Loops and two Bud Loops (in any order).

A finished 3-Bloom Unit is shown in **Photo 14**.

Photo 15 shows the 2-and 3-Bloom Units made for my Blooming Lavender. Notice that the placement of the Bloom Loops is varied.

Photo 15

Lavender

Leaves:

Wire: 26 gauge (.4 mm) lime green
Bead Color: C (lime green)

Bud Lavender: Make 10
Bloom Lavender: Make 10

Pattern: 1x 1 1/2 inch (3.8 cm) CL

Translation: Use the Continuous Loop technique to make just one loop using 1 ½ inches of beads for the loop.

Instructions:

1. String all the beads onto the wire.

2. Leave a 2 inch (5 cm) starting tail and a 1 inch (2.5 cm) ending tail. Twist the wire together only a few times below the loop. If you twist down further you will end up with more bumps on the flower stem. Leave the rest of the tail wire lengths untwisted, but trim them to different lengths—*this helps keep the flower stem more smooth and tidy*.

Photo 16

The finished Leaf is shown in **Photo 16**.

Assembly:

The Bud and Blooming Lavender will be assembled following the same procedure. My pictures show the Bud Lavender. To assemble the Blooming Lavender simply substitute six of the Bud Units in the pictures below for Bloom Units.

1. Prepare the stem wire by wrapping it with floral tape. *This tape layer adds extra grip to the stem wires which helps keep the units from sliding around on the slippery surface of bare wire.*

2. Cut several feet of embroidery floss. If you are using regular 6-ply embroidery floss, divide it into two 3-strand lengths to reduce bulk. *You can use floral tape to assemble the stems instead of floss. Cut several feet of tape from the roll, then cut it in half length-wise to make thinner tape. Using thinner tape helps reduce bulk on the stem wire and makes it easier fit the tape into small spaces between units.*

3. Lay a small tail of floss against the end of the prepared stem wire, then add in the Tip Unit directly at the tip of the stem wire. Wrap the floss around the flower stem wire, Tip Unit wires, and the starting tail of floss. Untwist the floss as you wrap so it lays flat. (**Photo 17**)

Photo 17

4. Continue wrapping the floss around the stem approximately ¼ inch (6.4 mm) below the Tip Unit.

5. Add in one Bud or Bloom Unit by wrapping the unit around the stem (**Photo 18**).

TIP: *You can always add in another length of thread if you run out while wrapping. Just lay the new thread's tail against the stem right below the last wrap, then wrap the tail of the old thread over it once. Hold onto the tail tightly and lay it against the stem, and continue with the new thread, making sure to wrap in the same direction as the old thread.*

Photo 18

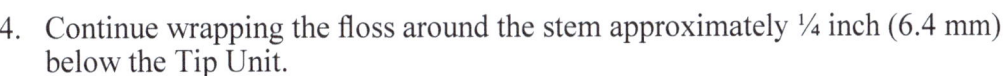

Lauren Harpster

Learn French Beading: Beginner Course

6. Wrap the longer tail wire around the last loop on the opposite end to close the unit around the stem. Do not twist the two wires together as this will make more lumps on the flower stem. Floss down below the unit approximately ¼ inch (6.4 mm) **(Photo 19)**

7. Repeat steps 5 & 6 until all of the units are attached to the stem. Spread the last two units approximately 1 inch (2.5 cm) apart. **(Photo 20)**

TIP: *As you wrap down the stem adding flowers, keep an eye on all the individual flower stem wires. If they start twisting around each other or the stem, straighten them before continuing. Otherwise, they will make unattractive lumps along the stem.*

Photo 19

8. Continue wrapping the floss 1 to 2 inches (2.5-5 cm) down the stem, then add in two leaves, one on the left and one on the right of the stem. **(Photo 21)**

9. Wrap approximately ½ inch (1.3 cm) down the stem, then rotate the stem 90 degrees and add two more leaves—one on each side of the stem **(Photo 22)**.

Photo 20   **Photo 21**   **Photo 22**

10. Repeat steps 8 & 9 until all five sets of leaves have been added to the stem. Rotating the stem between sets of leaves helps ensure the leaves fully encircle the stem. You are basically alternating between left/right and front/back positions. **(Photo 23)**

11. Continue wrapping the floss down the stem, at least to where the vase filler would meet the stem, then cover the end of the floss with floral tape to secure it.

Photo 23

47   BeadandBlossom.com

Lavender

Shaping:

Proper technique and assembly are just two parts of making French Beaded Flowers. The third part is shaping. In nature, flowers are generally not straight or flat, so to fully mimic them we need to mold our finished flower stems so they do not end up looking like little soldiers sitting in a vase. It really adds so much life to beaded flowers! **Always shape the flowers and leaves!**

Shaping the Lavender is simple. Start by bending and curling the leaves. Then add some gentle curves to the flower stem itself. You get to choose how much is enough. If you are making a larger arrangement, make sure the stems are not all shaped exactly the same. We are making flowers, not cookies. They should not look like they were all punched from the same mold. Check over the buds and blooms to make sure they are folded close to the stem, but not touching it. Bend the florets on the Bloom Loops so they face outward instead of upward.

Photo 24 shows some examples of finished Bud and Blooming Lavender.

Photo 24

Tips for Customizing the Design:

If you want your Blooming Lavender to be more full with more florets there are three options:

- Substitute more Bloom Units for the Bud Units.

- Replace the Bud Loops in the 2- and 3-Bloom Units with more Bloom Loops—up to 5 Bloom Loops total in each unit. You will need to increase the wire measurement for each of the Bloom Units.

- Mix the two options above. Make zero Bud Units and add extra Bloom Loops to each Bloom Unit.

For any of these options you will need to purchase extra beads and wire.

Photo 25 shows a Lavender using the first idea above. I made five 2-Bloom Units and five 3-Bloom Units. I also added a Bloom Loop in the Tip Unit.

- Make extra Bud and Bloom Units to make a taller flower head.

- You can leave off pairs of leaves at the bottom of the stem if they will be unseen below the lip of your vase.

Photo 25

Dame's Rocket

FLOWER HEAD SIZE: approximately 2 ¼ inches wide by 3 ½ inches tall (5.7 x 8.9 cm).

FLORET SIZE: approximately ¾ inch (1.9 cm) wide.

TECHNIQUES REQUIRED:
- Continuous Wraparound Loops
- Twisted Fringe
- Basic Frame
- Lacing

BeadandBlossom.com

This pattern will make one Small stem of Dame's Rocket (also called Dame's Violet) with 18 flowers and 3 leaves, or one Large stem with 25 flowers and 3 leaves. For my large arrangement I made two small stems and one large stem.

Dame's Rocket grows in shades of purple, pink, and white.

MATERIALS	SMALL STEM	LARGE STEM
SEED BEADS		
- 11/0 transparent color-lined pink (Color A)	25 grams	35 grams
- 11/0 opaque pale green or pale yellow for stamen (Color B)	< 1 gram	< 1 gram
- 11/0 transparent mint green (Color C)	20 grams	20 grams
WIRE		
26 gauge (.4 mm) copper core wire in petal color	30 ft (9.2 m)	45 ft (13.7 m)
24 gauge (.5 mm) lime green copper core wire	10 ft (3 m)	10 ft (3 m)
30 gauge (.25 mm) lime green copper core wire	12 ft (3.7 m)	15 ft (4.6 m)
16 gauge (1.23 mm) florist stem wire	1 piece	2 pieces
OTHER		
Light green floral tape	< 1 roll	< 1 roll
Green embroidery floss (optional)	~ 13 ft (4 m)	~18 ft (5.5 m)

FLOWER:

Wire: *26 gauge (.4 mm) petal colored wire*
Beads: *Colors A (petal) & C (mint green)*

Small Stem: Make 18
Large Stem: Make 25

Photo 1

Pattern: 4x 2 row CWL, 11-bead starting loop. Leave 6 beads before (4C, 2A) and 6 beads after (2A, 4C) the petals

Translation: Use the Continuous Wraparound Loop technique to make four petals. Each petal will have two rows of beads. The first row in each petal will be made of 11 beads. You need six beads on the wire in front of the petals strung in this order: 4 green, 2 petal. You need six beads on the wire after the petals in this order: 2 petal, 4 green.

1. Reserve ~1 gram (1.5 grams for a large stem) of Color A for the stamen and set them aside, then string the rest of Color A onto the 26 gauge wire. This will allow you to work from the spool without cutting lenghts of working wire.

2. String 4C onto the starting wire, then count out 2A from the spool. These beads will be left loose on the starting tail wire in front of the CWL petals. (**Photo 1**)

3. Leave a 3 inch (7.6 cm) tail wire (with the 4C and 2A beads on it), then work from the spool to make four petals as described in the pattern above. (**Photo 2**)

4. Close the unit into a circle by wrapping the working wire once around the first petal. Do not twist the tail wires yet.

Photo 2

Learn French Beading: Beginner Course

5. After closing the unit, count out 2A beads onto the working wire, then measure the working wire to 3 inches (7.6 cm) and cut from the spool.
6. String 4C onto the working end of the wire (**Photo 3**). Make small wire loops in the ends of the wires to make sure the beads don't fall off.

STAMEN:

Wire: *30 gauge (.25 mm) light green wire*
Beads: *Colors A, B, C*

Before you begin, string all of color B onto the wire. This allows you to work from the spool without cutting wire.

Small Stem: Make 18
Large Stem: Make 25

Pattern: 1x ⅛ - ¼ inch (3-6.4 mm) Twisted Fringe with 2 beads at the tip.

Translation: Use the twisted fringe technique to make a ⅛ inch (3 mm) twisted stem below two beads.

1. Count out 2B and slide them approximately ½ inch from the end of the starting wire.
2. Fold the wires on either side below the beads, then twist them together approximately ⅛ - ¼ inch below the beads. Clip off any excess starting tail wire. Measure the working wire to 2 inches (5 cm) then clip from the spool.
3. Add 2A then 4C to the working wire (**Photo 4**). Make a loop in the end of the wire to keep the beads from sliding off.

Photo 3

Photo 4

LEAVES:

Wire: *24 gauge (.5 mm) lime green, 30 gauge (.25 mm) lime green*
Beads: *Color C*

Before you begin, string all of Color C onto the 24 gauge wire. This allows you to work from the spool without cutting wire.

Small Leaves:
Small Stem: Make 2
Large Stem: Make 2

Pattern: 11 row BF, 1 inch (2.5 cm) BR, RB PT.
- **Reduce to two bottom wires**
- **Lace once across the center**

Translation. Use the Basic Frame technique. Make the basic row (row #1) 1 inch long. Wrap 11 rows total with a round bottom (90 degree wrap) and a pointed top (45 degree wrap). Once the rows are complete, reduce to two bottom wires by removing the working wire. The leaf will need to be laced.

1. Construct a basic frame as described in the pattern. The top wire should be about 1 inch (2.5 cm) long.
2. Wrap the remaining rows according to the pattern above.
3. After the last row, tie off the working wire and remove it by clipping it close to the stem wire. Clip the top wire short and fold it to the back of the leaf.
4. Cut approximately 4 inches (10.2 cm) of 30 gauge (.25 mm) lime green wire, and lace across the center of the leaf.

A finished Small Leaf is shown in **Photo 5**.

Photo 5

Dame's Rocket

Large Leaf:
Small Stem: Make 1
Large Stem: Make 1

Pattern: 13 row BF, 1 ¼ inch (3.2 cm) BR, RB PT.
- Reduce to two bottom wires
- Lace once across the center

Translation. Use the Basic Frame technique. Make the basic row (row #1) 1 ¼ inches long. Wrap 13 rows total with a round bottom (90 degree wrap) and a pointed top (45 degree wrap). Once the rows are complete, reduce to two bottom wires by removing the working wire. The leaf will need to be laced.

1. Construct a basic frame as described in the pattern above. The top wire needs to be about an inch (2.5 cm) long.
2. Wrap the remaining rows according to the pattern, then tie off the working wire and trim it close to the leaf stem wire. Trim and fold the top wire.
3. Cut approximately 5 inches (12.7 cm) of 30 gauge (.25 mm) lime green wire, and lace across the center of the leaf.

The finished Large Leaf is shown in **Photo 6**.

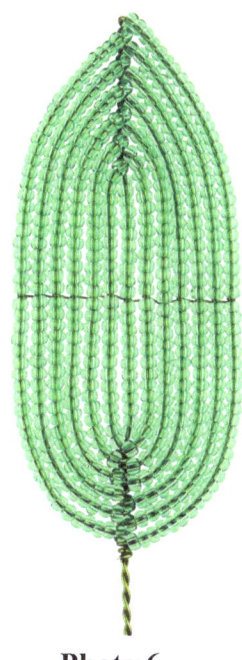
Photo 6

ASSEMBLY:

1. Wrap the 16 gauge florist stem(s) wire with a layer of floral tape to prepare the surface for assembly. *Floral tape gives the slippery stem wires more grip for a more secure assembly.*

Flowers:

1. Insert one stamen between the 2nd and 3rd petals (**Photo 7**). Position the two pale green or yellow stamen beads in the center of the flower, close to the surface.
2. Wrap bare stamen stem wire once around the base of the third petal to secure the stem beads in place.
3. Flip the flower over and slide all of the beads on the petal and stamen stem wires down against the bottom of the flower. (**Photo 8**)
4. Twist all three wires below the beads together approximately 1 inch (2.5 cm) down (**Photo 9**).

Photo 7

Photo 8

Photo 9

Learn French Beading: Beginner Course

Photo 12

Photo 11

Photo 10

5. Below the 1 inch twist, reduce the number of stem wires to one, by removing the 30g wire for the stamen and the shorter 26g wire. (**Photo 10**)

6. **Photo 11** shows an assembled flower. Repeat to make the other 17 flowers (25 total for Large Stem).

7. Cut a long length of floral tape in half length-wise to make thinner tape. *Thinner tape helps reduce bulk on the flower stem.* Wrap the stem wires on each flower with a thin layer of the half-width tape. To keep the layer thin, angle the tape downward so the tape will only overlap a little bit as you wrap (**Photo 12**). Rub your fingers over the stem wire to smooth out the floral tape.

8. Cut about 5 ft (1.5 m) of embroidery floss. If you are using regular cotton floss, divide the 6-strand thread into two 3-strand lengths. *Just like thinner tape, dividing the thread helps reduce bulk on the stem as well as improving the look of the floss wrapping.* If you are not wrapping the stem with floss, skip this step.

9. Press a small tail of thread against the flower stem, then wrap the thread around the flower stem, beginning just below the flower (**Photos 13 & 14**). *Untwist the floss as you wrap down to make a nice smooth wrap.*

Photo 13 **Photo 14**

Photo 15 **Photo 16**

10. Continue wrapping until the flossed section of stem is ½ - 1 inch (1.3 - 2.5 cm) long. Secure the end of the floss by tying one knot around the flower stem.(**Photo 15**)

11. Repeat for the rest of the flowers (17 more for small stem, 24 for large). (**Photo 16**) *Vary the length of the flossed section for the most natural results.*

Dame's Rocket

Small Flower Head:

Prep: Wrap the stem wires on the three leaves with half-width floral tape.

1. Cut approximately 8 ft (2.4 m) of embroidery floss. *You can work with shorter lengths of floss if you prefer, then add in extra thread as needed. See the assembly video for this flower for instructions on how to add in new thread.* If you are using regular cotton floss, divide the 6-strand thread into two 3-strand lengths. This floss will be used to attach all of the flowers to the main stem. *If you are not wrapping the stems with floss, use half-width of floral tape in it's place throughout all the assembly instructions.*

2. Press a small tail of the floss against the prepared 16g stem wire, then add two flowers to the end of the wire, lining up the last floss wraps on the individual flowers with the tip of the wire. Wrap the assembly floss around the flowers and 16g stem wire to attach them. (**Photo 17**)

Photo 17

Photo 18 **Photo 19**

3. Wrap the floss down ¼ inch (6.4 mm), then add in two more flowers on the opposite side of the stem. (**Photo 18**)

4. Wrap the floss down another ¼ inch (6.4 mm), then add in two more flowers on another side of the stem. (**Photo 19**)

5. Continue down the stem, adding in two flowers every ¼ inch (6.4 cm) along the stem until all 18 flowers have been added. You want to fully encircle the stem with flowers, not attach on just the left and right side, so add flowers where they will best fill in the flower head. (**Photo 20**)

NOTE: *As you wrap down the stem adding flowers, keep an eye on all the individual flower stem wires. If they start twisting around each other or the stem, straighten them before continuing. Otherwise, they will make unattractive lumps on the flower stem.*

Photo 20

6. After the last set of flowers, wrap the floss down another 1 to 2 inches (2.5 - 5 cm) then add in one Small Leaf directly against the stem. (**Photo 21**)

7. Wrap the floss down the stem another inch (2.5 cm) then add in the second Small Leaf on a different side of the stem wire. Wrap down another inch and add in the Large Leaf on another side of the stem. (**Photo 22**).

8. Wrap the floss down the stem until you reach the point that will be around an inch (2.5 cm) below the lip of your vase. As per a general rule in floral arranging, the full length of the flower stem should not be more than 1 ½ -2 times the depth of the vase. Measure your vase and consider how far above the vase you want the flowers to stick out. Use those measurements to determine how far down to wrap. Secure the end of the floss by tying one knot around the stem, then wrapping over the ends with floral tape.

Photo 21

Photo 22

Large Flower Head:

1. The Large Flower Head contains two stems of flowers: one made with eighteen flowers like the Small Stem above, and one smaller stem made with seven flowers. Follow the assembly instructions for the Small Stem to make these to flower heads without leaves. If you are flossing the stems, wrap the floss 2 - 2 ¼ inches (5- 5.7 cm) below the 18-flower head, and 1 - 1 ½ inches (2.5 - 3.8 cm) below the 7-flower head, and then tie off the threads. (**Photo 23**)

2. Use floral tape to combine the two stems below the floss wrapping. (**Photo 24**)

Photo 23

Photo 24

Dame's Rocket

3. Attach a new length of floss where the two stems join, then add the leaves in as you wrap down the stem, spacing them about 1 inch (2.5 cm) apart along the stem.

Photo 25 shows a finished Large Stem of Dame's Rocket. I chose not to floss the stem on this one so you can see the difference in appearance. Many artists use just floral tape to finish stems.

NOTE: *Dame's Rocket does also grow with fewer flowers than the small stem in this pattern, so it would be perfectly within the range of this species to make a smaller and shorter flower head.*

Shaping:

Always shape and mold beaded flowers to give them a little movement. Otherwise they look stiff.

For the Dame's Rocket, turn all of the flower heads so they face outward, except for the flowers at the tip, which should face upward. Bend some petals so the tips fold back. Shift flowers around as needed to fill in gaps. Gently bend the individual flower stems to give them a little bit of an arc. (**Photo 26**)

Bend, fold, and twist the leaves so they are not flat. Add some gentle curves along the stem. (**Photo 27**)

Photo 25

Photo 26   **Photo 27**

Lauren Harpster

Wild Clematis

TECHNIQUES REQUIRED:
- Continuous Loops
- Basic Frame
- Lacing

FLOWER SIZE: approximately 2 ½ inches (6.4 cm) wide.

This pattern will make one stem of Wild Clematis with 2 flowers and 6 leaves.

For my arrangement I made two standard sized stems with two flowers, and one smaller stem with just one flower.

This species of clematis is called Blue Virgin's Bower or Rock Clematis. It grows in shades of light blue, periwinkle, and light purple.

MATERIALS	AMOUNT
SEED BEADS	
- 11/0 opaque pale or light blue (Color A)	5 strands (~ 18 grams)
- 11/0 opaque white (Color B)	2 strands (~ 7 grams)
- 11/0 opaque pale green (Color C)	< 1 gram
- 11/0 opaque green rainbow (Color D)	7 strands (~ 26 grams)
WIRE	
24 gauge (.5 mm) light blue copper core wire	15 ft (4.6 m)
26 gauge (.4 mm) white copper core wire	6 ft (1.8 m)
24 gauge (.5 mm) green copper core wire	18 ft (5.5 m)
30 gauge (.25 mm) green copper core wire	10 ft (3 m)
16 gauge (1.23 mm) florist stem wire	4 pieces
OTHER	
Light green floral tape	< 1 roll
Light green embroidery floss (optional)	< 1 skein

STAMEN

Wire: *26 gauge (.4 mm) white copper core*
Beads: *White (B), pale green (C)*

Unit A
Make 2 (1 per flower)

Pattern: 7x CL using 21 beads (10B, 1C, 10B) per loop

Translation: Use the Continuous Loop technique to make 7 loops. Each loop will have 21 beads in this order: 10 white, 1 pale green, 10 white.

Photo 1

1. Cut approximately 16 inches (40.6 cm) of wire. Leave a 2 inch (5 cm) tail wire, then make loops according to the pattern above. (**Photo 1**) *You can pre-string the beads if you prefer to work from the spool.*

2. To close the unit, cross the working wire between the 2rd and 3rd loops and fold to the bottom. This should pull the last loop into the center. (**Photo 2**)

3. Wrap the starting tail wire around the 6th loop to close the last six loops into a circle around the 7th loop. (**Photo 3**)

4. Fold both wires to the underside of the unit and twist them together. Trim the working wire to 1 inch (2.5 cm). **Photo 4** shows the finished Stamen Unit A.

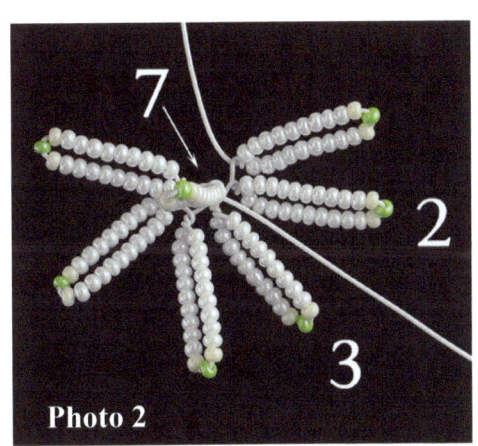

Photo 2

Photo 3

Photo 4

Lauren Harpster

Unit B:
Make 2 (1 per flower)

Pattern: 7x CL using 25 beads per loop, (12B, 1C, 12B)

Translation: Use the Continuous Loop technique to make 7 loops. Each loop will have 25 beads strung in this order: 12 white, 1 pale green, 12 white.

1. Cut approximately 18 inches (45.7 cm) of wire. Leave a 2 inch (5 cm) starting tail wire then make the loops according to the pattern above. (**Photo 5**)
2. Close the unit into a circle by wrapping the working wire around the first loop, then twisting the two wires together below the unit. **Photo 6** shows a finished Stamen Unit B.

Photo 5

Photo 6

Petals:
Wire: 24 gauge (.5 mm) light blue
Beads: *Light or pale blue (A)*

Before you begin, string all of color A onto the 24 gauge spool of wire. This will allow you to work from the spool without measuring or cutting any wire.

Make 8 (4 per flower)

Pattern: 7 row BF, 1 inch (2.5 cm) BR, PB PT
- **Reduce to two bottom wires**

Translation: Use the Basic Frame technique to make a petal that is 7 rows wide. The Basic Row (row #1) needs to be 1 inch long. Wrap all rows with a pointed bottom (45 degree wrap) and a pointed top (45 degree wrap). After the last row, remove the working wire.

1. Construct the basic frame as described in the pattern. There are only 7 rows, so the Top Wire only needs to be about ¾ inch (1.9 cm) long.
2. Wrap the remaining rows according to the pattern. Tie off the working wire by wrapping it a couple times just below the last row of beads, then carefully clip it close to the stem wire.
3. Cut the bottom loop open and twist the two bottom wires down approximately 1 inch (2.5 cm). Leave the rest of the wires untwisted, but cut them to different lengths. *This method of trimming wires helps the flower stem taper down in size, rather than having an abrupt change in stem thickness.* Trim the top wire and fold it to the back of the petal.

Photo 7 shows a finished Petal.

Photo 7

Wild Clematis

LEAVES:

Wire: *24 gauge (.5 mm) green, 30 gauge (.25 mm) green*
Beads: *Green (D)*

Before you begin, string all of color D onto the 24 gauge spool of wire.

Photo 8

Small Leaf
Make 4

Pattern: 11 row BF, 3/4 inch (1.9 cm) BR - RB PT
- **Reduce to two bottom wires**
- **Lace once across the center**

Translation: Use the Basic Frame technique to make a leaf that is 11 rows wide. The Basic Row (row #1) needs to be ¾ inch long. Wrap all rows with a round bottom (90 degree wrap) and a pointed top (45 degree wrap). After the last row, remove the working wire. The leaf will need to be laced.

1. Construct a Basic Frame as described in the pattern above. The Top Wire above the Basic Row should be around 1 ½ inches (3.8 cm) long.

2. Wrap the remaining rows according to the pattern.

3. Tie off the working wire below the leaf, then carefully trim it close to the stem. Twist the two bottom wires down about 1 inch (2.5 cm), and leave the rest of the wires untwisted. Trim the two bottom wires to different lengths. Cut the top wire to ¼ inch (6.4 mm) then fold it to the back of the leaf.

4. Cut approximately 4 inches (10.2 cm) of 30 gauge (.25 mm) green wire and lace across the center of the leaf.

Photo 8 shows the finished Small Leaf.

Large Leaf
Make 2

Pattern: 15 row BF, 1 inch (2.5 cm) BR - RB PT
- **Reduce to two bottom wires**
- **Lace once across the center**

Translation: Use the Basic Frame technique to make a leaf that is 15 rows wide. The Basic Row (row #1) needs to be 1 inch long. Wrap all rows with a round bottom (90 degree wrap) and a pointed top (45 degree wrap). After the last row, twist the working wire into the two bottom wires. The leaf will need to be laced.

1. Construct a Basic Frame as described in the pattern. The Top Wire above the Basic Row should be at least 1 ¾ inches (4.5 cm) long.

2. Wrap the remaining rows according to the pattern.

3. Tie off the working wire below the leaf, then carefully trim it close to the stem. Twist the two bottom wires down about 1 inch (2.5 cm), and leave the rest of the wires untwisted. Trim the two bottom wires to different lengths. Cut the top wire to ¼ inch (6.4 mm) then fold it to the back of the leaf.

4. Cut approximately 6 inches (15.2 cm) of 30 gauge (.25 mm) green wire and lace across the center of the leaf.

Photo 9 shows a finished Large Leaf.

Photo 9

Assembly:

Prep:

1. Wrap all four stem wires with a layer of floral tape to prepare the surface for assembly. *The layer of tape gives the slippery surface of the wire more grip for a more secure assembly.*

2. Cut a long length of floral tape in half length-wise to make thinner tape. Use this tape to wrap a thin layer on each leaf and petal. *Just like the stem wire, wrapping with tape provides better grip. Using thinner tape helps reduce the bulk on the flower stem.*

Leaf Branches:

1. Cut a long length of light green embroidery floss. If you are using regular 6-ply cotton thread, divide the thread in half to make two 3-strand threads. Lay a small tail of floss against the stem of a Small Leaf. Wrap the floss around the leaf's stem wire, beginning just below the leaf. *Untwist the floss as you wrap so the individual threads lay flat against the stem.* (**Photo 10**).

2. Wrap the floss down the leaf stem approximately ¾ inch (1.9 cm). Tie one knot in the thread around the stem to secure it. Lay the ending tail of thread flat against the leaf stem below. (**Photo 11**)

3. Repeat for the second Small Leaf, then set them both aside. Do not floss the large leaf stem.

4. Place the tip of a prepared 16g stem wire at the base of the Large Leaf, with the leaf's stem wire on top of the 16g stem. Use half-width floral tape to wrap the leaf stem to the 16g stem. (**Photo 12**)

Photo 10   **Photo 11**

Photo 12

Photo 13

5. Wrap down approximately 1 inch (2.5 cm) then add in two Small Leaves, one on each side of the stem. Both of the Small Leaves should have a ¾ inch (1.9 cm) long stem (the same length as the floss wrapping). (**Photo 13**)

6. Wrap the tape to the end of the stem. *Make sure the leaf stem wires do not twist around the 16g stem wire.*

7. Repeat to make a second Leaf Branch.

Wild Clematis

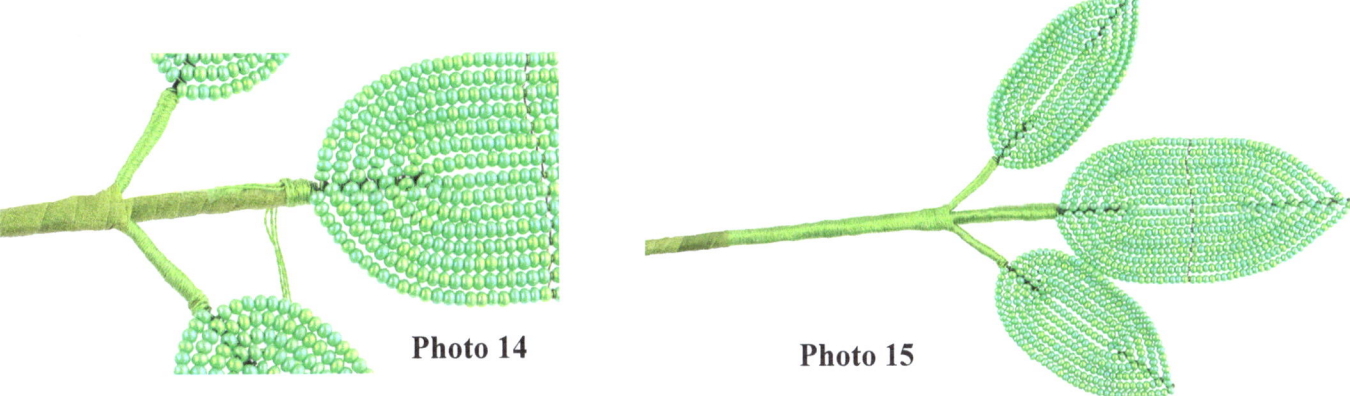

Photo 14 Photo 15

8. Cut another long length of floss and divide it into 3 strands. Attach one of the threads directly below the Large Leaf. (**Photo 14**)

9. Carefully wrap the floss down the leaf branch. Gently bend the Small Leaves back once they start getting in the way, then bend them back into place once you've wrapped below them.

10. Wrap to approximately 2 ½ inches (6.4 cm) below the Small Leaves, then either tie off the thread or secure it by wrapping over the tail with floral tape. (**Photo 15**)

Flowers:

1. Insert the stem wire of Stamen Unit A into the center of Stamen Unit B. (**Photo 16**)

2. Pull Unit A stem wire all the way through, then twist all of the stamen stem wires together. **Photo 17** shows a finished Stamen. Use half-width tape to wrap the stamen's stem wire.

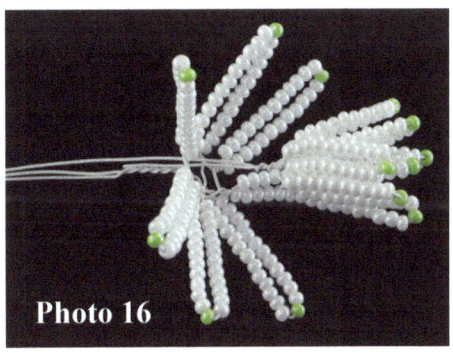

3. Shape each of the petals like **Photo 18**. Add a little curve right at the base of the petal, then bend the stem wire back sharply. Note that the back of the petal is on the inside of the curve. Set them aside.

4. Use half-width tape to attach the completed Stamen to the end of one prepared 16g stem wire (**Photo 19**). Wrap the tape just to the end of the stamen stem wire, making sure to keep the stem wires straight and untwisted as you wrap down.

Photo 18

Lauren Harpster

Learn French Beading: Beginner Course

5. Cut approximately 2 ft (61 cm) of 30 gauge green wire. Add two petals directly below the stamen and hold them in place, once on each side. The back of the petals should be facing the stamen. Lay a small tail of the 30g wire against the stem directly below the stamen and petals. Tightly wind the long end around the stem and petal stem wires 3 or 4 times, keeping the wraps high and directly below the petals. (**Photo 20**)

6. Keep holding the first two petals with one hand, then add two more petals with the other hand. Position the new petals between the first two so they fully encircle the stamen. Tightly wind the long end of the 30g assembly wire around the two new petals 3 or 4 times to secure them to the flower stem. (**Photo 21**)

TIP: *This type of assembly where you wire on petals one or two at a time is something you will see often with Basic Frame petals. One key point with this type of assembly is to not let go of the stem wires until they are completely secure (after step 7 below).*

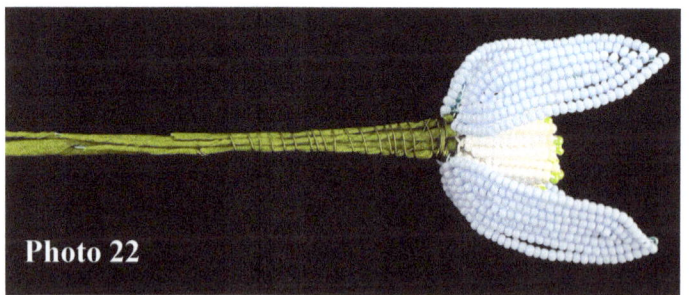

7. Continue wrapping the assembly wire down the stem, at least 1 inch (2.5 cm) below the flower head, slowly moving your hand that should still be holding the petal stem wires down the stem as needed. (**Photo 22**) *Make certain that the individual petal stem wires do not twist around each other or the flower stem. This will make lumps on the flower stem.*

8. Take a look at the petal stem wires. To ensure that the flower stem tapers down in width gradually, rather than getting thin abruptly, trim the petal wires to varying lengths.

9. Cover the exposed wire wrappings with a layer of floral tape. It does not matter this time if it's half-width or full-width. (**Photo 23**)

10. Repeat to make the second flower.

11. Cut several feet of embroidery floss and divide it in half.

Wild Clematis

12. Just like the leaf branches, attach one of the threads directly below the flower head, then wrap the floss down approximately 6 inches (15.2 cm) for one flower, and 8 inches (20.32 cm) for the second flower. Secure the ends of the floss by wrapping over it with floral tape. (**Photo 24**)

13. Gently bend the stem wires directly below the flower heads to make the flowers face downward.

Photo 25 shows the face of a finished flower.

Photo 24

Photo 25

Photo 26

Combining the Stems:

1. Using floral tape or floss, attach one Leaf Branch and the shorter Flower to the longer Flower stem. The stems should join where the floss wrapping ends. (**Photo 26**). Wrap the tape to the end of the stems, making sure they do not twist around each other as you tape down.

2. Trim the longer stem wires as necessary so they are all the same length as the shortest stem wire.

3. Cut more floss and divide it. Attach it to the stem just below the joint of the three individual stems and wrap down about an inch (2.5 cm) (**Photo 27**). Secure the end of the floss by wrapping over it with floral tape.

4. Just below the floss wrapping, add in the second Leaf Branch and wrap the tape to the end of the stems (**Photo 28**). Trim the stem wire so it is the same length as all the others.

5. Attach another length of floss and wrap down to just below where the stem will meet the lip of the vase. If you are unsure, wrap down at least 2 inches (5 cm) for security.

Photo 27

Photo 28

Shaping:

Just like every other flower that I've taught so far, you absolutely MUST shape and mold the petals, leaves, and stems. I cannot stress enough how important this is to creating life-like flowers.

To shape the petals, gently curl just the tips outward or inward - *use a mix of both! Don't make all the flowers and petals the same!* Twist a couple of the petals just slightly. You don't need to be extreme here, just enough so they aren't flat and straight. If any rows bow outward or separate from the petal while you are shaping them, carefully mold them back into place. On this plant, the flowers always droop down toward the ground. (**Photos 29 & 30**)

To shape the leaves, bend them, curl them, twist them, fold them. Like most Clematis, this plant is a vine. So add as many curves and bends to the leaf stems as you like. Flower stems are generally straight, with the exception of the bend near the flower head. (**Photo 31**)

Photo 29   **Photo 30**   **Photo 31**

Photo 32

When making a larger arrangement of flowers that have multiple stems of the same flower, vary the configuration of the stems. Wait to trim the stems until you're ready to arrange so you have some room to adjust the height while you're arranging the flowers. Move the leaf branches to different locations, but always at least 5 inches (12.7 cm) below the flowers for this Clematis. Vary the amount of flowers or leaves. This makes the arrangement more interesting and natural.

For my full arrangement I made two stems with two flowers and one stem with one flower like the one shown in **Photo 32**.

Black-Eyed Susan

TECHNIQUES REQUIRED:
- Continuous Loops
  - Centering the Stem Wire
  - Reinforcing Continuous Units
- Continuous Crossover Loops
- Basic Frame
- Lacing

FLOWER SIZE: Approximately 3 inches (7.6 cm) wide

Lauren Harpster

Learn French Beading: Beginner Course

This pattern will make one stem of Black-Eyed Susan with two flowers, one bud, and five leaves.

For my arrangement I made two of the standard sized stems, and one stem with one flower and one bud.

Materials	Amount
Seed Beads	
11/0 opaque luster yellow (petals)	40 grams
11/0 transparent dark brown (stamen)	10 grams
11/0 transparent green (leaves & sepals)	40 grams
Wire	
24 gauge (.5 mm) gold colored copper core wire	25 ft (7.6 m)
24 gauge (.5 mm) green copper core wire	30 ft (9.1 m)
30 gauge (.25 mm) green copper core wire	< 5 ft (1.5 m)
26 gauge (.4 mm) brown copper core wire	10 ft (3 m)
16 gauge (1.23 mm) florist stem wire	3 pieces
Other	
Green floral tape	< 1 roll
Green embroidery floss (optional)	1 skein

Stamen:

Wire: *26 gauge (.4 mm) brown copper core*
Beads: *dark brown*

Before you begin, string all of the brown beads onto the wire. This allows you to work from the spool without measuring or cutting wire.

Unit A:
Make 3 (1 per flower, 1 per bud)

Pattern: 7x 9 bead CL

Translation: Use the Continuous Loop technique to make seven loops. Each loop should have nine beads.

1. String the brown seed beads onto the wire.
2. Leave a 2 inch (5 cm) tail wire, then make the loops according to the pattern. (**Photo 1**)
3. Measure a 2 inch (5 cm) tail and cut from the spool.
4. To close, cross the working tail wire over the unit between the second and third loops. (**Photo 2**) Pull the wire tight, which should pull the last (7th) loop into position in the center of the unit.
5. Wrap the beginning tail wire once around the sixth loop to close the first 6 loops into a circle around the last loop. (**Photo 3**)

Photo 4 shows the finished Unit A

Photo 1   Photo 2

Photo 3   Photo 4

Black-Eyed Susan

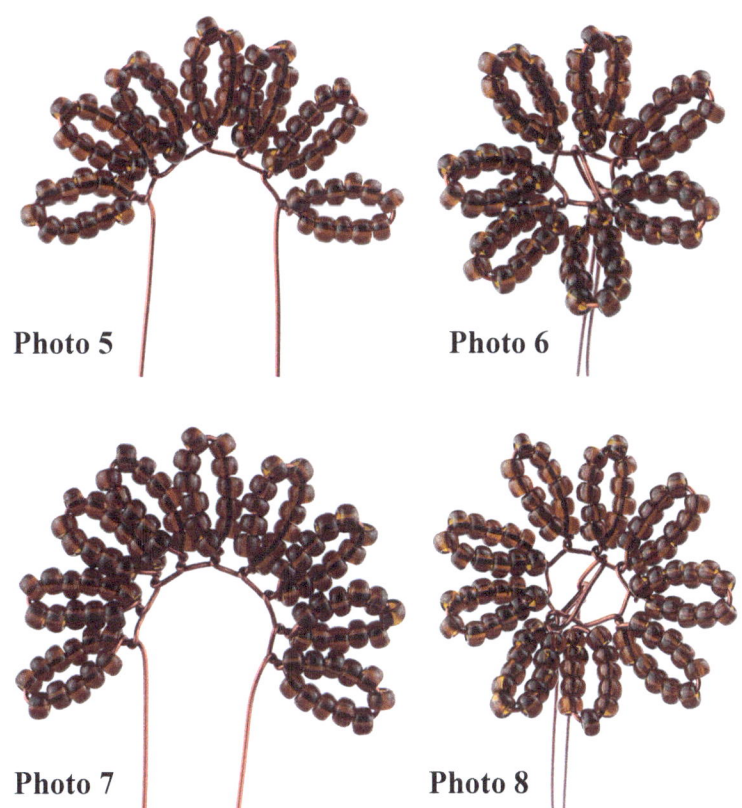

Photo 5 Photo 6
Photo 7 Photo 8

Unit B:
Make 3 (1 per flower, 1 per bud)
Pattern: 7x 11 bead CL

Translation: Use the Continuous Loop technique to make seven loops. Each loop will have eleven beads.

1. Leave a 2 inch (5 cm) tail wire, then make the loops according to the pattern. (**Photo 5**)
2. Close the unit by wrapping the working wire once around the first loop, then centering the wires below. Twist the two wires together, then cut the working wire to about 2 inches (5 cm).

The finished Unit B is shown in **Photo 6**.

Unit C:
Make 7 (3 per flower, 1 per bud)
Pattern: 9x 11 bead CL

Translation: Use the Continuous Loop technique to make nine loops. Each loop should have eleven beads.

1. Leave a 2 inch (5 cm) tail wire, and make the loops according to the pattern. (**Photo 7**)
2. Close the unit and center the stem wires below. Twist the two wires together, then cut the working wire to about 2 inches (5 cm).

The finished Unit C is shown in **Photo 8**.

PETALS:
Wire: *24 gauge (.5 mm) gold colored copper core*
Beads: *yellow*

Before you begin, string all of the yellow seed beads onto the wire.

Flower Petals:
Make 4 (2 per flower)
Pattern: 7x CCL using 3 inches (7.6 cm) of beads for the starting loop.

Translation: Use the Continuous Crossover Loop technique to make seven petals. To start each petal, make a starting loop out of 3 inches of beads.

Photo 9

1. Leave a 2 inch (5 cm) starting tail wire, then make the loops according to the pattern above.
2. Close the unit into a circle. Reinforce the unit by wrapping the working wire around the base of each petal, and then twist the wires together at the side of the unit.

A finished Flower Petal Unit is shown in **Photo 9**.

Lauren Harpster

Learn French Beading: Beginner Course

Photo 10

Bud Petals:
Make 1
Pattern: 10x CL using 2 inches (5 cm) of beads per loop.

Translation: Use the Continuous Loop technique to make ten loops. Each loop should be made from 2 inches of beads.

1. Leave a 2 inch (5 cm) starting tail wire, then make the loops according to the pattern above.
2. Close the unit into a circle and center the unit stem wires below.

The finished Bud Petal Unit is shown in **Photo 10**.

Sepals:
Wire: *24 gauge (.5 mm) green copper core*
Beads: *11/0 transparent green seed beads*

Before you begin, string all of the green seed beads onto the wire.

Flower Sepals:
Make 2 (1 per flower)
Pattern: 10x CL using 2 inches (5 cm) of beads per loop.

Translation: Use the Continuous Loop technique to make ten loops. Each loop should be made from 2 inches of beads.

Photo 11

1. Leave a 2 inch (5 cm) starting tail wire, then make the loops according to the pattern above.
2. Close the unit by wrapping the working wire around the first loop. Do not center the unit stem wires.

The finished Sepal Unit is shown in **Photo 11**.

Photo 12

Bud Sepals:
Make 1
Pattern: 8x CL using 1 ½ inches (3.8 cm) of beads per loop.

Translation: Use the Continuous Loop technique to make eight loops. Each loop should be made from 1 ½ inches of beads.

1. Leave a 2 inch (5 cm) starting tail wire, then make the loops according to the pattern above.
2. Close the unit by wrapping the working wire around the first loop. Do not center the unit stem wires.

The finished Bud Sepal Unit is shown in **Photo 12**.

Leaves:
Wire: *24 gauge (.5 mm) green, 30 gauge (.25 mm) green wire to lace*
Beads: *size 11/0 green seed beads*

Black-Eyed Susan

Small Leaf:
Make 3
Pattern: 13 row BF, ¾ inch (1.9 cm) BR, PB PT.
- **Three bottom wires**
- **Lace once across the center**

Translation: Use the Basic Frame technique to make a leaf with 13 rows across. The Basic Row (row #1) should be ¾ inch long. Wrap at a 45 degree angle at the bottom and top wires to make a Pointed Bottom and Pointed Top. Twist the working wire into the two bottom wires to make three bottom wires. Lace the leaf once across the middle.

1. Construct a Basic Frame using ¾ inch (1.9 cm) of beads for the Basic Row. The top wire should be at least 1 ½ inches (3.8 cm) long.
2. Wrap rows 2-13 with a pointed bottom and pointed top, then twist the working wire into the bottom wire and cut from the spool. Trim and fold the top wire.
3. Cut approximately 5 inches (12.7 cm) of 30 gauge green lacing wire and lace across the center of the leaf.

A finished Small Leaf is shown in **Photo 13**.

Photo 13

Large Leaf:
Make 2
Pattern: 15 row BF, 1 inch (2.5 cm) BR, PB PT.
- **Three bottom wires**
- **Lace once across the center**

Translation: Use the Basic Frame technique to make a leaf with 15 rows across. The Basic Row (row #1) should be 1 inch long. Wrap at a 45 degree angle at the bottom and top wires to make a Pointed Bottom and Pointed Top. Twist the working wire into the two bottom wires to make three bottom wires. Lace the leaf once across the middle.

1. Construct a Basic Frame using 1 inch (2.5 cm) of beads for the Basic Row. The top wire should be at least 1 ¾ inches (4.5 cm) long.
2. Wrap rows 2-13 with a pointed bottom and pointed top, then twist the working wire into the bottom wire and cut from the spool. Trim all of the bottom wires to varying lengths. Trim and fold the top wire.
3. Cut approximately 6 inches (15.2 cm) of 30 gauge green lacing wire and lace across the center of the leaf.

A finished Large Leaf is shown in **Photo 14**.

Photo 14

Assembly:

Flower Stamen:

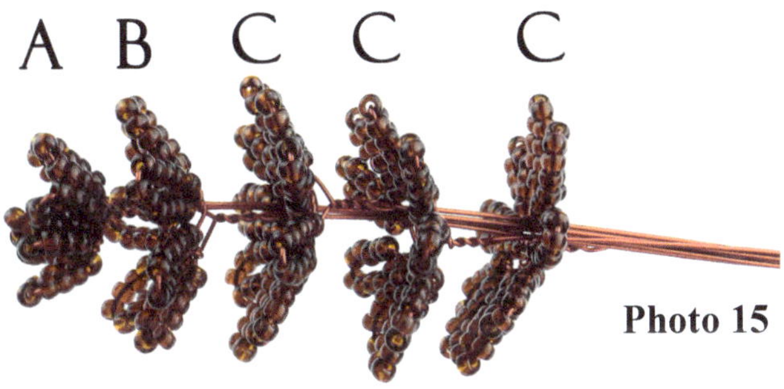

1. Insert the stem wire of Unit A into the center of Unit B. Then insert the combined unit stem wires into the center of three Unit C's, one at a time. **(Photo 15)**

Photo 15

2. Carefully check the units and rotate them as necessary to keep the sides of the "dome" even. Then twist the unit stem wires all together.

Lauren Harpster

Learn French Beading: Beginner Course

Photo 16

Photo 17

3. The finished Flower Stamen is shown in **Photo 16**. Repeat to make the second flower's stamen.

Bud Stamen:

1. Follow the same procedure as the Flower Stamen to make the Bud Stamen, using 1x Unit A, 1x Unit B, and 1x Unit C.

The finished Bud Stamen is shown in **Photo 17.**

Bud:

1. Wrap one 16 gauge (1.3 mm) stem wire with floral tape to prepare the surface for assembly.

2. Cut a long length of floral tape in half lengthwise to make thin tape. Use this thinner tape to wrap a thin layer of floral tape on each of the stamen. *Using thinner tape helps reduce bulk on the stem.*

Photo 18

3. Insert the end of the prepared 16 gauge stem wire into the underside of a Stamen. Use a length of thin floral tape to attach the stamen to the stem wire. (**Photo 18**)

4. Insert the bottom end of the stem wire into the center of the Bud Petals and Bud Sepals and bring them all the way up below the stamen. (**Photo 19**)

5. Push the petals and sepals as close to to the stamen as possible. Cut around 2 feet (~60 cm) of 30 gauge green wire. Lay a small tail of wire against the stem, then, starting just below the sepals, wrap the wire tightly around all of the component wires and stem wire. Wrap down at least 1 inch (2.5 cm) (**Photo 20**)

Photo 19

Photo 20

Photo 21

6. Cover the exposed wires with a layer of floral tape.

7. Cut another foot of 30 gauge green wire, and use it to attach 1x Small Leaf 2-3 inches (5 - 7.6 cm) below the flower head. (**Photo 21**)

8. Cover the exposed wires with floral tape.

9. Cut several feet of embroidery floss. If you are using regular 6-ply embroidery thread, divide the thread into two 3-strand lengths.

Black-Eyed Susan

10. Just like the assembly wire, lay a small tail of the floss against the stem directly below the sepals. Hold the tail in place while you wrap the long end of the floss over it. (**Photo 22**)

11. Continue wrapping down the stem, being careful to lay the floss directly beside the previous wraps to ensure you get full coverage. Untwist the thread as you wrap to make sure it lays flat.

12. As you come to the leaf, gently bend it backwards so you can wrap floss directly above it, then fold it back into place while you wrap underneath it.

13. Wrap the floss 1-2 inches (2.5-5 cm) below the leaf, then trim it to a couple of inches (5 cm). Lay the tail of the floss against the stem, and wrap over it with floral tape to secure it. (**Photo 23**)

Photo 22

Photo 23

Photo 24

14. Don't forget to shape the petals, sepals, and leaf! Curl some of the petals inward toward the stamen. Bend some outward so they look like they're starting to unfold. Do the same thing with the sepals. Curl some up around the sides of the bud, while bending the others down. Twist, bend, and crinkle the leaf so it doesn't sit flat. This shaping is such an important part of making beaded flowers look alive.

The finished Bud is shown in **Photo 24**.

Flowers:

1. Wrap the stem wires on the Flower Stamen with half-width tape. Attach a Flower Stamen to the end of one of the prepared 16 gauge florist stem wires just as it was done for the bud. (**Photo 25**)

2. Cut around 2 feet (~60 cm) of 30 gauge green wire for assembly.

3. Insert the bottom end of the stem wire into the center of two Flower Petal Units and one Flower Sepal Unit (**Photo 26**) and push them up against the bottom of the stamen.

Photo 25

Photo 26

Lauren Harpster

Learn French Beading: Beginner Course

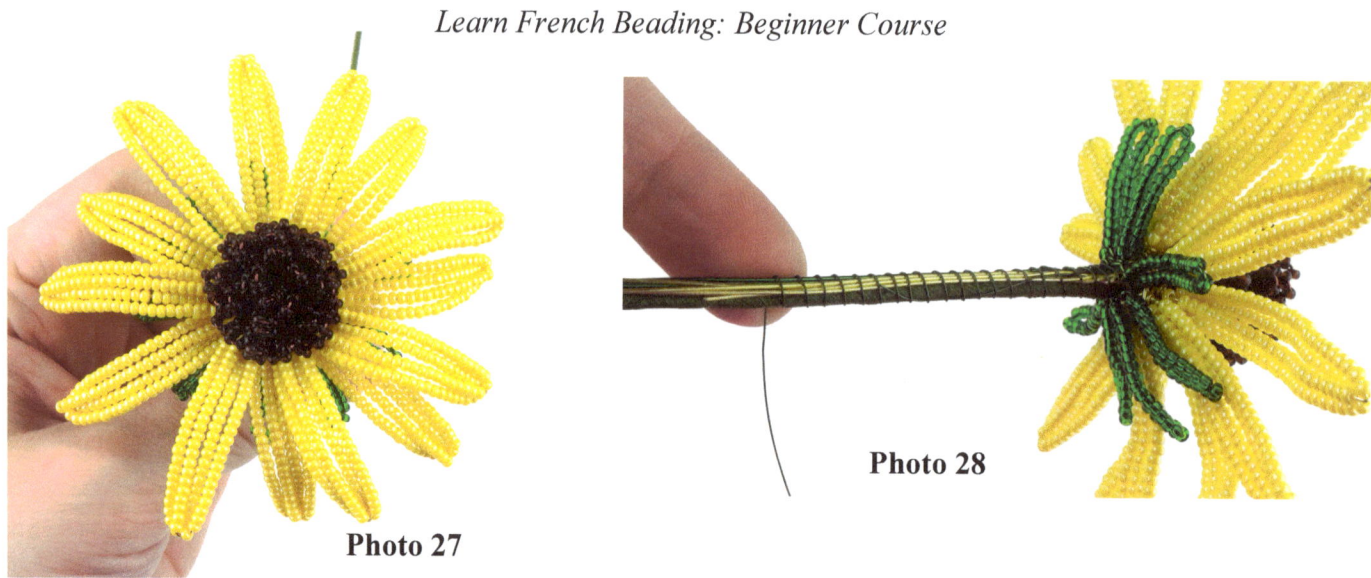

Photo 27

Photo 28

4. Rotate the petal units until the petals in the top unit are between the petals in the lower unit and not directly on top of them. (**Photo 27**)
5. Use the 30 gauge assembly wire to attach the petal and sepals securely to the flower stem. (**Photo 28**)
6. Cover the exposed wires with a layer of thin floral tape to prepare for the next assembly layer.

Photo 29

Photo 30

7. Approximately 2-3 inches (5-7.6 cm) below the flower, attach one Small Leaf with around 2 feet (~60 cm) of 30 gauge green wire. (**Photo 29**)
8. Continue wrapping the wire down the stem 1-2 inches (2.5-5 cm), then add in a Large Leaf on the opposite side of the stem (**Photo 30**). Cover the exposed wires with half-width floral tape. *Using thinner tape here will help you get into those tight cracks between the leaf and flower stem.*
9. Cut several feet of embroidery floss and wrap the stem down to approximately 2-3 inches (5-7.6 cm) below the Large Leaf.
10. Repeat to make a second Flower. You can vary the placement of the leaves on the second Flower to make a more natural and interesting looking combined flower stem.

A fully assembled flower is shown in **Photo 31**.

Photo 31

Black-Eyed Susan

Photo 33

Photo 32

Combining the Stems:

1. Line up the bottom of the floss wrapping on the two flowers. Use floral tape to attach them together below the floss wrapping (**Photo 32**). *The flowers do not need to be the same height.*

2. Use more floral tape to add in the bud. (**Photo 33**)

3. Trim all the flower stem wires to be the same length as the shortest one.

Photo 34

4. Attach another length of embroidery floss where all the stems meet, and wrap down another inch or two (2.5-5 cm) - just to where the stem would meet the vase lip (**Photo 34**). *If your Black-Eyed Susans will not be in a vase, or if the stems will be fully exposed, wrap the floss all the way down to the end, then use a bit of glue (I like Fabri-Tac) to secure the ends of the floss.*

Shaping:

Generally I only do basic shaping before the final stage of assembly. Once the full stems are put together, I go back through and add more detailed shaping. You can add as much or as little of the shaping as you want, but do shape it in some way. There is more than one way to shape a Black-Eyed Susan correctly. Some have drooping petals, while others' petals are more straight, or even curving upward. I encourage you to play with your petals until you are happy with the way they look. Here's how I shaped mine.

1. Bend the petals near the base so they droop downward. (**Photo 35**)

Photo 35

Learn French Beading: Beginner Course

Photo 36 Photo 37 Photo 38

2. Look over the petals one by one. On some of them, bend just the very tips outward, while curling other petal tips even further inward toward the stem. Pick a few petals to twist gently. All of these bends create movement, which is crucial in making stiff bead-and-wire flowers look more natural. (**Photo 36**)

3. Repeat the same process on sepals beneath the flower head. If the rows of beads separate during shaping, carefully mold them back together. (**Photo 37**)

4. Bend, curl, and twist the leaves so they aren't flat. (**Photo 38**)

5. Don't forget to add some gentle curves to the stems. Flowers rarely have straight stems.

Photos 39 - 41 show all of the Black-Eyed Susan stems that I made for my arrangement. Note that they are not all in the exact same configuration with the same heights or number of flowers. Having a variety of stems makes a larger arrangement more natural and interesting.

Photo 39 Photo 40 Photo 41

BeadandBlossom.com

Part 4
Arranging Beaded Flowers

Learn French Beading: Beginner Course

Selecting Flowers

I knew when I started planning this course that I wanted a wildflower theme. When you look out over a field of wildflowers, you get a nice mix of color. Wildflowers don't care about color schemes, they just grow wherever their seeds fall. Following this idea, I decided that I wanted a mix of colors to capture that aesthetic.

Besides having a mix of colors, I also wanted a mix of shapes. A dozen roses is beautiful and classic, but I feel a mixed bouquet holds the attention longer because there's more to see. The Black-Eyed Susan is a round, ray-shaped flower. The lavender is tall and slender, adding streaks of purple throughout the bouquet. The Dame's Rocket has a wonderful stalk form with multiple florets forming the flower head. And finally, the Wild Clematis has those lovely cup-shaped, drooping heads. This mix of shapes not only gave my bouquet a more organic feel, but also allowed me to teach multiple types of assembly.

While making the flowers, I intentionally made each of the stems of the same flowers with a different configuration. Some have extra flowers, some have less flowers. Leaves aren't always in the same spots. I do recommend when making a bouquet like this one that you don't make every stem of the same flower exactly the same. In nature, flowers don't all grow the same.

Selecting Beads

Another part of making beaded flowers and arrangements is the selection of beads. Unfortunately, this isn't an aspect of design where there are hard, fast rules that will apply across the board. *What works for one arrangement might not work for another. What works for one artist may not suit another.* I designed the Black-Eyed Susan first, and as I tested that flower I decided the opaque luster bead emulated the flower the best. Other types of beads just seemed so dull for such a happy flower. Then, as I tested the other flowers I made them in multiple finishes. Some of them looked great in other finishes! However, when I combined the flowers together, some seemed more muted in comparison with the flowers that I made in opaque beads. This is because opaque beads tend to be more bold than other types of beads. I didn't want any one flower to take over the bouquet by being bolder and brighter than the rest, so I made them all in some type of opaque bead to match the boldness. But they aren't all the same type of opaque finish. I did use a mix of opaque luster, opaque, color-lined - which have a similar enough affect, and opal - which are a semi-opaque bead. *One thing I can say for certain, opaque beads tend to pop out in a design, while transparent beads tend to sink into the background. So if there are any details you want to call* extra *attention to, either in a single flower or a whole bouquet, make those details in some type of opaque beads. Your eyes will be drawn there first.* Part of my bead selection was also determined by what was easily available in the colors I needed.

The leaves were a completely different story. Most flowers have green leaves. However, when you put a lot of one bead color together, it tends to form an indiscernible mass of color. You loose all the little details that make the leaves unique and interesting. You lose the outlines and shapes because your eyes can't see the edges of individual leaves. So, I intentionally used multiple tints of light and dark greens *and* different finishes: opaque, opaque rainbow, transparent, transparent luster. *When you're making an arrangement, mix your greens! This same principle applies when you're making an arrangement where the flowers have a monochromatic scheme.* If I had made the Beginner Course bouquet in all yellow, for example, I would have used multiple types and shades of yellow - some opaque, some transparent, some matte, etc, to prevent the loss of detail. *In these cases, mixing finishes and tints within the same color family makes a big difference.*

BeadandBlossom.com

Selecting a Vase

There are a few points to keep in mind when picking out a vase for your flowers. French beaded flowers tend to be top-heavy, so picking a vase with a wider bottom is beneficial to keeping it from toppling over. An arrangement with a larger number of flowers will require a wider vase than an arrangement with fewer flowers. Likewise, consider the width of the opening in the vase. An arrangement with fewer flowers probably won't look as nice in a vase with a wide mouth.

A *general* rule of thumb in floral arranging is that the total height of the flower stems should be no more than 1 ½ to 2 times the height of the vase. I chose a vase that is 7 inches (17.8 cm) tall, allowing for flower stems up to *around* 14 inches (~36 cm). But I highly recommend not trimming any flower stems until you start arranging them in the vase. This allows you room to play with the placement and height.

Because this is a wildflower bouquet, I didn't want a vase that was too formal-looking, so I searched for something with a more cottage feel. I found a galvanized, silver-colored pitcher that I thought would give me the look I wanted, as well as having a wide base and opening. Then I painted it because the silver was too dull next to the bright flowers (**Photo 1**).

Photo 1

Arranging the Bouquet

I didn't want my wildflower bouquet to look heavily "manicured". However, because the flowers are handmade and not plucked at random from a field, I wanted to make the most of my time and efforts in making them, so I did plan a few things.

In my *non-professional florist* mind, there are two basic types of arrangements - arrangements that are visible on all sides, like a centerpiece, or backless arrangements that are placed against a wall or shelf so only the front and sides are visible. Through the process of designing, recording, and photographing I ended up with multiples of each flower stem. So I decided to make a centerpiece. If your arrangement will be set up against a wall, you probably won't want to put flowers on the back of the display where they will be unseen. That's just a waste of beads and work! Consider where you will be displaying the bouquet and go from there.

Photo 2

First, I filled the vase with glass marbles to a few inches below the rim. These act as both a counter-weight against the flowers, and a way to hold flowers in place inside the vase.

I started with the Black-Eyed Susans, spacing them around the vase (**Photo 2**). Notice that they are not all the same height, and they are facing different directions. While I want the arrangement to be interesting on each side, I don't want each side to be identical. Having yellow distributed at different heights within the bouquet draws the eye from one part of the bouquet to another. Plus, in nature, flowers of the same type don't always grow to the same height, so we also have a more natural and organic placement. Also note that the flowers aren't all turned to show their faces. Some have profile views or show their undersides.

Learn French Beading: Beginner Course

Then I added in the Dame's Rocket. Just like the Black-Eyed Susan stems, I wanted these pink bunches of flowers at different heights and placements within the bouquet, and I wanted some pink visible on all sides. (**Photo 3**)

I noticed as I was arranging that most of my greenery was below the flowers, which traps the green down low. Varying the height of the stems helps a bit with that, but, the way the leaves are configured on the Clematis stems gives me an opportunity to lift some of that greenery up between the flower heads. So I've left one stem tall and positioned it in the center of the arrangement so it's leaves are taller and higher up. Just like the previous flowers, I wanted some blue visible on all sides. **Photos 4 & 5** show two different sides of the arrangement. On one side the Black-eyed Susans were up high, and I needed something low, so I put my single flowered clematis there. On the other side I left it at mid-height. Basically, fill in the gaps between the other flowers.

Photo 3

Photo 4

Photo 5

Photo 6

The lavender stems are the easiest to add in. Just poke them into the arrangement between other flowers to add little pops of purple. It's okay to put two closer together, since we're going for a wild look. But do vary the height on these as well. I left one very tall to help keep the taller blue clematis company. **Photos 6 & 7** show the arrangement with lavender added.

This arrangement uses marbles only to keep the flowers steady. The downside to this way of displaying beaded flowers is that flowers can shift around. If the vase is knocked over you'll have to redo your arrangement. The good thing about this kind of arrangement is that it's not permanent, and it's really easy to change things around or add new flowers.

Photo 7

Arranging Beaded Flowers

Alternate Method for Making Bouquets

Instead of inserting individual stems into marbles to hold them steady, you can use floral tape to attach all the flowers together into a bouquet. With this method, you will end up with one stem at the bottom of the arrangement. Because the flowers are all attached together, it's very easy to move from one vase to another, and the flowers won't shift around or get knocked out of place. However, it will be harder to change the arrangement itself or add in more flowers.

To begin, fill the vase with marbles. They are still needed to hold the bouquet stem still and act as a counter-weight against the top-heavy flowers. Arrange the flowers in the vase as you'd like them to look in the finished arrangement. Look through the instructions on the previous page for ideas. Planning out the arrangement beforehand will help you get all the flower stems to the desired length, which will make assembling the bouquet easier. Just keep in mind that once you tape the flowers together, they will be pulled closer together than how they appear in the vase. Use a camera or phone to take a picture of the arrangement from all sides. These will be a great reference so you can double check the placement of flowers while you're assembling.

To assemble the bouquet, start in the middle and work your way outward in rings. Take out a few flowers in the very center of the arrangement. Use floral tape to wrap the stems together (**Photo 8**). Don't wrap the tape too far up the stems. Keep in mind the depth of the vase, and let the flowers have a little room to breathe below the last leaf. Remove the next row of flowers from the center of the arrangement. Use another layer of floral tape to add them in around the center flowers *one or two stems at a time* (**Photo 9**). Since you have already planned the arrangement in the vase, you can match up the bottoms of the stems with the flowers in the center to get the proper height.

Photo 9

Photo 8

Photo 10

Continue building outward in rings until you've added in all the flowers (**Photo 10**). Then you can simply insert the single bouquet stem into the marbles in the vase.

This is the same way that I assemble wedding bouquets! All you would need to add is a ribbon wrapping around the stem. For a wedding bouquet of this style, I would recommend making the wrapped section of stem no more than 7 inches (17.8 cm) long.

More Sample Arrangements

You don't have to make a large amount of flowers to have a nice arrangement. I know many first-time French Beaders making these flowers may only make one or two of each, or perhaps will not want to make every type of flower. So I've put together some other arrangements with the flowers for inspiration.

Photo 11 has a little bit of each flower- one stem of Black-eyed Susans, three blooming stems of Lavender, two Dame's Rocket stems, and one Wild Clematis.

Photo 12 is just Black-eyed Susans and Lavender.

Photo 13 has one large and one small stem of Dame's Rocket and one large and one small stem of Wild Clematis.

Photo 11   **Photo 12**   **Photo 13**

Resources

Because I live in the USA, most of the shops that I have actually used are located in the US. However, I have also added some sources that I know of in other countries. I have browsed the sites to see if materials are available there, but have not purchased from them.

Seed Beads:

USA
Fire Mountain Gems - *firemountaingems.com*
Shipwreck Beads - *shipwreckbeads.com*
Beaded Edge Supply - *beadededgesupply.com*
Orr's Trading Post - *orrs.com*
Pow Wow Supply - *powwowsuppy.com*
Aura Crystals - *auracrystals.com*
Caravan Beads - *caravanbeads.com*
Eureka Crystal Beads - *eurekacrystalbeads.com*
Fusion Beads - *fusionbeads.com*

UK
GJ Beads - *gjbeads.co.uk*
Spellbound Beads - *spellboundbead.co.uk*
Spoilt Rotten Beads - *spoiltrottenbeads.co.uk*
The London Bead Company - *londonbeadco.com*

Canada
Bead FX - *beadfx.com*
Beazu - *beazu.ca*
Butterfly Beads - *butterflybeads.ca*
I-Bead - *www.ibeadcanada.com*
That Bead Lady - *thatbeadlady.com*

Wire:

USA
- Parawire - *Parawire.com, UnkamenSupplies.com*
- Artistic Wire - *Beadalon.com, Shipwreckbeads.com, GreatCraftWorks.com*
- Zebra Wire - *Firemountaingems.com*
- Paddle Wire - *local craft or florist supply store*
- Florist Stem Wire - *Papermart.com, local craft or florist supply store*
- Galvanized Steel Wire Coils - *local hardware store, Amazon.com*

UK
Scientific Wire - *wires.co.uk*

Other Supplies:

Any store with a floral department should have a selection of foam, moss, marbles, floral tape, and other potting and assembly needs.

- Embroidery floss - *local craft store, DMC.com, JEC.com* (for flat untwisted silk floss)
- Non-hardening Clay & Plaster - *local craft store, Amazon.com, dickblick.com*

More Tutorials & Patterns:

My website has many more technique lessons, as well as my free and paid patterns and my blog. - BeadandBlossom.com

Historical References:

- Levi, Ragnar. *Flower Forever: Bead Craft from France and Venice.* 2015.
- Crabb-Edwards, Jonalee A. (2001) *Origins of Beaded Flowers.* View at http://www.Roxelana.com/new/papers/origins-of-beaded-flowers.

Lauren Harpster

Glossary

A -

Assembly - The process of attaching flower pieces to a stem to make a completed flower.

B -

Basic Frame - A French beading technique with two axis wires. Rows of beads are wrapped along the two axis wires around a center row of beads.

Basic Row - The center row on a Basic Frame. When counting rows, this is row number 1.

Basic Wire - Another name for the Top Wire on a Basic Frame.

Bead Spinner - A tool used to string beads onto wire. It is comprised of a bowl, a spindle, and a base.

Bottom Wire - The lower axis wire on a Basic Frame. The twisted section of wire below the Basic Row.

Branching Fringe - A type of compound wire-back fringe that makes coral-like fringes.

C -

Continuous - A term that means multiple petals/sepals/leaves will be made on one single length of wire.

Continuous Crossover Loops - A French beading technique that begins with a starting loop of beads, and another loop of beads that crosses over the front and down the back of the starting loop.

Continuous Loops - A French beading technique that creates a series of simple beaded loops.

Continuous Wraparound Loops - A French beading technique that begins with a starting loop of beads, with more rows of beads wrapped around the starting loop.

Copper-core Wire - The type of wire used to make the flower components. This wire has a copper core that is plated with other metals or coated in other colors. It is not the same as copper wire.

E -

Embroidery Floss - Cotton or flat silk threads used to wrap flower stems for a nicer finish.

F -

French Beading - A term used to describe a specific set of techniques used primarily to make flowers. The art combines seed beading, wire wrapping, and sculpture.

Flossing the Stem - The act of wrapping flower stems with embroidery floss.

Floral Tape - A special type of paper tape used to assemble and finish flower stems.

Florist Stem Wires - A type of steel wire that can be used as flower stems.

Fringe Loops - A French Beading technique that combines continuous loops with a wire-back fringe to make a loop with a fringe in the middle of the loop.

G -

Galvanized Steel Wire - A type of wire that can be used as flower stems.

Gauge - A term used to describe wire diameters commonly used in the United States. The smaller the number, the thicker the wire.

H -

Hank - A bundle of threads strung with beads with the ends knotted together at the top.

I -

Immortelle - A mourning wreath made from French Beaded Flowers. These were popular memorials during the late 1800's and early 1900's.

L -

Lacing - Sewing across a petal or leaf with fine wire to help hold rows tightly together.

Lace-as-you-go - Lacing while constructing the petal or leaf instead of after.

Loop-Fringe - A French Beading technique that combines continuous loops and wire-back fringe to make a loop at the tip of a fringe.

P -

Pointed Bottom - A term in a pattern that tells you to wrap at a 45 degree angle at the bottom wire of a Basic Frame or Continuous Wraparound Loop unit to make a point in the bottom of the leaf or petal.

Pointed Top - A term in a pattern that tells you to wrap at a 45 degree angle at the top wire of a Basic Frame to make a point in the top of a leaf or petal.

R -

Reverse Wrap - Wrapping at the top or bottom wire of a Basic Frame by crossing over the back first. The result is the exposed wire wraps showing along the top wire on one side of the petal, but on the opposite side of the petal, the wraps show along the bottom wire.

Rocaille - Another name for a round seed bead.

Round Bottom - A term in a pattern that tells you to wrap at a 90 degree angle at the bottom wire of a Basic Frame or Continuous Wraparound Loop unit to make a rounded edge at the bottom of the leaf or petal.

Round Top - A term in a pattern that tells you to wrap at a 90 degree angle at the top wire of a Basic Frame to make a rounded edge on the top of a leaf or petal.

S -

Seed Beads - Small glass beads that look like donuts. The type of bead used to make French beaded flowers.

Starting Loop - The center or beginning loop in a Continuous Crossover Loop or Continuous Wraparound Loop petal.

Stem Wire - Refers to either the stem wire of a flower, or the individual stem wires on petals and leaves.

T -

Top Wire - Part of the Basic Frame. The axis wire directly above the Basic Row. Also called the Basic Wire.

Twisted Fringe - A French Beading technique that makes a single bead or small loop of beads on a long twisted wire stem.

U -

Unit Stem Wire - The stem wires on a petal, leaf, or continuous unit. Used to attach flower components to the flower stem.

W -

Working Wire - The long end of wire, usually strung with beads, that is used to make rows around a basic row, or starting loop.

Lauren Harpster

Technique Abbreviation List

BF - Basic Frame
BR - Basic Row
CL - Continuous Loops
CCL - Continuous Cross-over Loops
CWL - Continuous Wraparound Loops
RB - Round Bottom
RT - Round Top
PB - Pointed Bottom
PT - Pointed Top
RW - Reverse Wrap

BeadandBlossom.com

About the Designer

My name is Lauren Harpster, and I am the designer at Bead & Blossom. I live in Utah with my husband and our three children. I have been making and designing French Beaded Flowers for almost nine years. For me, this is more than just a craft or a hobby, it's a calling!

I've been publishing my beaded flower patterns for almost six years, and I've developed several new techniques in that time. In 2017 I published my first book "French Beading Patterns: Christmas Collection". While I have been teaching the art through my website for many years, this "Beginner Course" is my first full course that is combined with video instructions. I am thrilled to be able to make this resource available to share my experiences with everyone who wants to learn this amazing art.

Me holding my "Color Wheel Wreath" - a project I made one piece each day for the year 2018

Above: Rose and Berry Wedding Bouquet
Left: Azalea Topiary
Both by Lauren Harpster

The berry patterns are from "Beaded Berry Collection", a design collaboration between myself and my friend Suzanne Steffenson.

OTHER BOOKS BY THIS DESIGNER

- French Beading Patterns Volume 1: Christmas Collection (December 2017)

BeadandBlossom.com

www.ingramcontent.com/pod-product-compliance
Lightning Source LLC
Chambersburg PA
CBHW042247100526
44587CB00002B/48